SIX VOWELS AND TWENTY-THREE CONSONANTS

SIX VOWELS
AND
TWENTY-THREE CONSONANTS

AN ANTHOLOGY OF
PERSIAN POETRY
FROM
RUDAKI TO LANGROODI

edited, translated and introduced by
Ali Alizadeh & John Kinsella
with a Preface by Kenneth Avery

Arc
PUBLICATIONS
2012

Published by Arc Publications
Nanholme Mill, Shaw Wood Road
Todmorden, OL14 6DA, UK
www.arcpublications.co.uk

Design by Tony Ward
Printed by Lightning Source

ISBN: 978 1906570 57 6

The publishers are grateful to the authors and, in the case of
previously published works, to their publishers for allowing
their poems to be included in this anthology. They would
particularly like to thank Caravan Books Publishing House,
Teheran, for granting permission to use poems from *Hezar-o
yek sh'er* (Caravan Books, 2007) in the second section of this
anthology. Some of these translations have been previously
published in *Landfall, Poetry Review, Salt, Southerly* and *Warwick
Review*. The publishers would also like to thank Nick Sheerin
for his work on the typesetting and lay-out of this book.

Cover image: 'Cosmos 20' (mixed media) by Marcos Grigorian
in the Teheran Museum of Contemporary Art

Arc Publications 'Anthologies in Translation'

CONTENTS

Preface Kenneth Avery / 9
Introduction – John Kinsella / 11

I
CLASSICAL PERSIAN VERSE
Introduction – Ali Alizadeh / 19

RUDAKI / 25
from divan-e rudaki / 26

FERDOWSI / 29
from the shah-nameh / 30
from the shah-nameh / 32

OMAR KHAYYAM / 35
Three quatrains from the Rubaiyat / 36

BABA TAHER / 39
Three Quatrains / 40

MAHASTI / 43
Four Quatrains / 44

ATTAR / 49
from the Mantegh at-Tayr / 50
from the Mantegh at-Tayr / 52

NEZAMI / 55
from Haft Peykar / 56

SAADI / 59
from the Golestan / 60
quatrain from the Divan-e Saadi / 60

RUMI / 63
ghazal from Divan-e Shams-e Tabrizi / 64
from the Masnavi Ma'navi / 66

HAFEZ / 69
ghazal from Divan-e Hafez / 70
ghazal from Divan-e Hafez / 72

Jami / 75
from Haft Awrang / 76

Vahshi Bafqi / 81
Ghazal / 82

Hatef Esfehani / 85
Ghazal / 86

Tahirih Qorrat al-Ayn / 89
Ghazal / 90

II
MODERN PERSIAN POETRY
Introduction – Ali Alizadeh / 95

Nima Yushij / 99
The Phoenix / 100

Parvin Etesami / 105
The Tear of the Orphan / 106

Shahriar / 109
from 'Alas, My Mother' / 110

Ahmad Shamlu / 117
The Journey / 118

Fereydoon Moshiri / 123
The Nights of Karun / 124

Simin Behbahani / 129
You Said It's a Grape / 130

Mehdi Akhavan-Sales / 133
The Return of the Ravens / 134

Nosrat Rahmani / 137
Exile in a Ring of Chains / 138

Forough Farrokhzad / 143
The Bird, Only a Bird / 144

Tahereh Saffarzadeh / 147
Fog in London / 148

Ahmad-Reza Ahmadi / 151
The Absence of Contact / 152

Mimi Khalvati / 155
Ghazal – after Hafez / 156

Partow Nooriala / 157
Woman / 158

Mahmoud Kavir / 165
Come With Me to Lebanon / 166

Ali Zarrin / 171
Free Ghazal (1) / 172

Mahasti Shahrokhi / 175
Beautiful Wounds / 176

Shole Wolpé / 179
High Above Tehran / 180

Davood Salehi / 181
Untitled 3 / 182

Farzaneh Ghavami / 185
The Same Events / 186

Mandana Zandian / 189
Untitled / 190

Alireza Behnam / 193
Hanging from the Trees of Babylon's Temple / 194

Bahareh Rezai / 197
48 / 198

Ahmad Zahedi Langroodi / 201
Thread of the Noose / 202

About the translators / 205

Poetry in the Persian language has a long and distinguished history. After the Arab Islamic conquests of the seventh and eighth centuries had dealt a death blow to the Iranian languages associated with Zoroastrian religion and the Sassanian empire, the 'new' Persian language began to be written in Arabic script and borrowed Arabic words. It was no accident, however, that the first great work in this 'new' Persian was the long epic poem of Iranian nationalism, the *Shah-nameh* or 'Book of Kings' by Ferdowsi. This tenth / eleventh century 'world history' culminated in the valiant battles for the Iranian homeland before the coming of Islam.

In fact, the ninth and tenth centuries saw an efflorescence, a true renaissance of linguistic creativity in the Iranian sphere, a reawakening of the indomitable spirit of Iran, not only in poetry and literature, but in all the civilized arts, philosophy, science and spirituality. This 'rebirth' made an immense contribution to Islamic and Middle Eastern culture generally, and has continued through the pre-modern period down to today.

Poetry was always the preferred literary form adopted by Persian writers wherever there has been the influence of Iranian culture. This is true for the great 'classical' period of Saadi and Hafez, as much as for the later developments of the Safavid and Mughal periods in the eastern Persian-speaking lands. On the Indian subcontinent, classical Persian and its daughter-language Urdu were the chief poetic vehicles well into the twentieth century and the end of the British Raj. Today, poets writing in Farsi continue the great traditions of the past, though there are many new and exciting ways in which this ancient craft is being reshaped.

Much of this splendid history is unknown to the English-speaking world. It is true that we have many translations of Rumi or even Hafez, and of course Edward Fitzgerald's creative adaptation of Omar Khayyam. But this is more part of the West's romanticising of the East, where we have made poets such as Khayyam or Rumi in our own image as reflections of our romantic or 'new age' yearnings.

Why should we concern ourselves with the Persian poetic tradition, when other 'national' languages and cultures have much to offer? The reason lies not in nationalist feeling alone, but in the other great and dominant motif of Persian poetry, its spirituality, in particular, the spirit of Sufism. No other culture in the world has produced such quantity and quality of mystical poetry and true spiritual vision as the Persian tradition. This rich source of splendour is present not only in the real poetic visionaries, in Rumi, Hafez, Attar, Jami, and many others, but inhabits and permeates all literary efforts of Persian writers. In this poetry there is an effulgence of meaning; nearly every word resonates with chords of allusion and multiple signification. Whether we read a modern poet or one of the classics, this resonance reaches back to the beginnings of the tradition, and it touches us today.

The poems and translations in the present volume represent just a sample from this perennial stream. From the austere nationalist pride of Ferdowsi we move to the honeyed poise of the classical and post-classical lyricists, with their measured rhyme and meter. The most exciting and deeply affecting verse in this anthology, however, is from the twentieth-century poets, with their intense personal feeling and freedom of expression. Influenced by Western literary styles, many of these writers share our modern concerns, but there is also an underlying starkness, a concern with the brutality and violence so sadly a part of the twentieth-century experience. Yet all the poets represented here conjure up the culture and people of Iran in a dazzling way.

Persian poetry should be heard, recited and read aloud in the company of friends, lovers and wine. That these latter are forbidden by the life-denying regime in power today is one of the paradoxes for all those who respect Iranian history and traditions. But this makes these poems and the stream from which they flow all the more relevant. In being put into English by such able translators, we can glimpse the beauty of the originals, and for some of us, that glimpse and vision of life is never enough. As Rumi sang, paradoxically,

> I am silent. Speak, O soul of soul of soul,
>   from desire of your face, every atom began to speak.

Kenneth Avery

WHERE I SIT IN THE PROCESS: WORKING WITH ALI ALIZADEH TO PRODUCE AN ANTHOLOGY OF PERSIAN POETRY

The conversations that have gone on between Ali Alizadeh and myself over how best to render Persian poetry, selected from over a thousand years of writing, into English-language poems, run to many hundreds of pages. After three years of swapping emails and versions of poems, we feel ready to offer this volume to readers. Though anthologies are by their very nature reductive, we feel this is by no means a narrow selection. We have tried to step outside the usual safety zones of Persian-into-English poetry and, in doing so, to challenge the status quo of the industry of making Persian poetry digestible for capitalist Western audiences, who might look for solace and spiritual affirmation through often ecstatic and mystical poems that seem to offer an alternative to the materialism and apparent meaninglessness of modern existence.

This is the first of many deceptions we wish to expose. There has been exploitation, and misrepresentation, in saccharine and overly lush renderings of, for example, Rumi, into modern Englishes, to placate the desire for a spiritual heal-all at one's bedside, yet still to enjoy the pleasures of Western materialism (the 'having one's cake and eating it too' school). True, Rumi is big enough to stand on his own two feet, and translation is about taking liberties, making a text relevant to the time and space it is to be read in. But such wilful construction of a mediaeval master to suit all tastes in consumer society, as a way of offsetting that society's spiritual deprivation, is disingenuous to say the least.

Such translations increase in times of imperialist capitalism. The mid-to-late nineteenth century was one such boom, coming out of Victorian Britain's empire-building and resolving of ancient cultures into museum fodder to entertain the steadily-rising middle class, and to 'amaze' the threatening working class into reverence for the captors, collectors and collators of such materials. Another surge was post- the Iranian Revolution, which for obvious reasons American translators took as a stimulus to the 'real' spiritual and poetic integrity of Persian civilisation. In essence, the spikes in Persian translation, or Iranian works, old and new, coincide with creating an alternative to the Islamic state version that holds sway. While these kinds of usages are inevitable and deplorable, one can also state that present-day Iran is no easy place for a poet to practise, and state oppression there is absolute.

This is not to speak on behalf of the contemporary Iranian poets included within this volume, as they negotiate their own paths within the state, and each will have their own views on this, but to declare an outsider's view of isolation and enclosure, while noting that the tyranny is not only internal but also applied by countries outside Iran. Essentially, in collecting a volume of this sort, one is laid open to the charges of either being supportive of a pariah state, or opposing it. In my case, I see all states as oppressive, all nations as contradictions of freedom and liberty. Iran's oppressions may be more overt than others, but all states share such qualities.

This book, from my point of view, is a book about the dynamics of poets working in their own space, against social, political, spiritual and environmental backdrops. It is not about me (or Ali) stating a political position *per se*, but, nonetheless, we are aware that we occupy and make such a position through the act of participation. This makes translation more than a conversion of words, an approximation, a version, or a departure. It makes it an act of codification and code-breaking, and if we are to steer clear of the militaristic associations of these words, which is our express desire, then every word and every line translated has to be done in an informed way. We have attempted to keep the translations as close to the original as possible. We have selected pieces that don't push nationalist bandwagons, though at the same time they reflect nationalist issues and cultural identity in the context of the individual poet's identity. National myths of origin and status cannot be ignored, but they can be accorded a less prominent place. Suffering is a given, and poets never escape it. There is suffering across various regimes. If poets can't speak, then the darkness is overwhelming and hope is lost.

One of the major issues for two poets in translating dozens of poets of both genders and across a thousand-year period, is the risk of making all in the same tone – that is, imposing the translators' tone. While this can never be entirely avoided, both Ali and I have gone for an understated 'exactness' rather than a mystical liberation of often already-liberated texts. It is poetry of one language, and poetry with a cultural familiarity regardless of era or gender. Issues are different, the body has its own rules, but there is a conversation between poets and poems across the ages.

In the twentieth-century Persian poets, we find an awareness of their same-language predecessors and traditions, but also a growing awareness and interaction with, say, other modernist poets. As we move through the modern period, discourse with the greater poetic world increases, unsurprisingly. Isolated, Iranian poets have created a language of simultaneous connection and disconnection, and seem to speak among themselves, most importantly, before speaking outwards. Diaspora poets often write of their own isolation outside Iran, and their acts of textual resistances take on complicated roles in affirming their own liberties while lamenting the lack for those in their 'home' country. This is a fraught issue, as an apologia for Western capitalist exploitation as 'better' than the obvious abuses of religious fundamentalism becomes a binary opposition, and one that doesn't work. Unless the diaspora poet is critiquing his or her own privilege, the act of liberation through text becomes compromised. In the end, the few pieces by diaspora poets we have included have been chosen because they seem not to fall into this trap, by our estimation.

Translation processes differ for me depending on context and familiarity with a specific language. Latin-script languages are far easier for me to work with: I have translated a lot from the French, but also from other European languages. I do not have Farsi, and find it hard to follow, and though I am learning as I go, and seeking to gain an understanding of the language, I am largely relying on Ali Alizadeh's literal English versions. But it's not simply a case of 'converting' this to an 'English-language' poem. There's clearly a process of collaboration: I ask Ali to send me the literal rendering, together with a commentary on the poem itself, on the poet, and any technical / prosodic peculiarities. Ali is a fine poet and an acute reader of poetry, and passionate about Persian/Iranian poetry – as I have become myself – it is one of the great world poetries. I also ask him to send me a copy of the original: I like not only to see the shape of the poem on the page, but to do my best with the script, and with understanding how it is working. It is also important for me to get historical and cultural contexts for the poem, whether of the past or contemporary. As my familiarity with the language has grown, so has my ability to make use of the originals.

In the end, though, it is an inherent 'sense' of the poem that makes it work – some poems I cannot translate, others really find their mark with me. Once I have done my first version, I send it back to Ali for comment. I usually have a few points to query regarding possible meanings of words – variations, subtleties and so on – and broader technical questions. Ali sends back comments and reactions with possible alternative interpretations. I have found he does this more frequently when I am reworking 'classical' or medieval Persian poetry, than when it is contemporary Farsi poetry – I naturally feel more kinship with the latter and tend to 'get' the poetry and poetics more readily. I enjoy working, though, and as someone with a bit of a 'history' background, I like to explore eras and contexts.

A few of the technical questions that confronted me, in making choices from Ali's roughs, concerned whether to retain rhyme, the connected issue of refrains, whether to preserve basic word order or rearrange, and whether to maintain certain characterising prosodic elements, especial of the *ghazal*. Interestingly, these issues changed with time, and towards the latter stages of the process, I tended towards maintaining as many of the original impositions (or rules) as possible. Consistent concerns revolved around retaining the *qaafiyaa* (rhyme) and *radif* (line-end word repetition) or not, along with the more easily achieved usage of the poet's name (*takhallus*) in the last couplet (*bayt*) of the poem. Various experiments were conducted with meter, but meter is most often what I varied to equate with more open-form English-language poetics. Certainly, in the modern poems, the phrase became as much the standard as the line, and the residue of earlier techniques (especially out of the couplet, heroic couplet, quatrain and the *ghazal* itself), is played against free verse and more open forms.

Particularly with classical poems, I found myself taking slight liberties that could seem great liberties to some. For example, one of my comments back to Ali regarding a Nezami translation went:

> Taken some liberties with this. I have gone for 'the word' (Russian formalism!) and have utilised 'knowledge' (Sufi?!) etc…. and changed some of the singular / plurals….

Or, wrestling with the great Attar:

> This was real tough, Ali. I have provided some options/queries in the right margin. Regarding 'animated' – I see it more as illumined from what I get of Sufism, but I might be entirely wrong. Go back to that if it's closer. Once again, great liberties. I went for 'wander' because of the spiritual and literary associations it carries, and because it takes a bit of the agency away. Probably wrong!

This doesn't mean we stuck with these decisions, but it's the kind of conversation that took place. And here's a reply from Ali regarding a Rudaki translation:

> …maybe 'touch' would actually be better than 'hold' in the last line. The Persian word *gereftan* (roughly: to get) is very

flexible; but I think hold might be too strong, although I do like its association with 'hand' through alliteration. I guess the thing with touch is that it could be accidental – perhaps? – and I think the 'getting' of the beloved's sleeve here is quite deliberate. I'm thinking maybe something like 'caress', or 'stroke', even 'feel'? catch? I love 'of yours' rhyme. Perfect.

And so the exchanges would flow until we both reached a version that satisfied us. Sometimes this could take many exchanges; sometimes it was much quicker. Issues of alliteration and rhyme (I wanted to understand exactly how the rhymes for '*qays*' worked, for example, even if I chose not to go down that path), and especially metrics, were constantly raised. Maybe, however, the most significant issues of discussion were to do with cultural register. I think respect is the most important attribute in a translator when representing a language's poetry, a process that seemingly homogenises great difference when one should in fact be scrupulous in avoiding such generics – respect keeps this at the forefront of thought.

Here's a message / query from me to Ali that touches on such issues:

> …is religion the same as faith in this context – I guessed the comparison was one between status quo 'religion' and a faith / spirituality that transcended this (Sufi)? Also, do the internal commas work within the dynamic of the original (i.e. the hiatus) – I got the impression from earlier quatrains by other 'early' poets that this might be a problem – if not, great… it expands the syntactical possibilities. One of the reasons I have not done complete reinterpretations (more versions) and recastings is to try and retain the basic movement of the originals. If we can be more interpretive then it expands horizons – but then, overall, that might create problems of 'trust' re readers and this kind of anthology?

And, in the end, this anthology rests on issues of trust – from the poets, from the readers, and between ourselves. For me, Persian poetry helps give reason for existence.

John Kinsella

I
CLASSICAL PERSIAN VERSE

As with any other narrative, the story of Persian poetry predates the narrative's designated beginning, and will certainly stretch beyond the termination of its telling in a single volume. Persian poetry, from its appearance in the early Middle Ages to its continuation beyond the present and into the future, defies the basic duration of our account as presented in this anthology. Yet, for the sake of presentation and accessibility, we have divided this phenomenon into two broad, semi-chronological categories: classical and modern.

Such a classification is, of course, rather problematic. It may seem to smack of, for example, a Eurocentric attitude – shaped by a certain version of European history that sees history in terms of an absolute opposition between the milieus of the *ancien régime* and those of a progress towards moral and cultural perfection – or it may convey a naïve belief in modernity's efficacy to supplant classical / traditional values and usher in an entirely new epoch of, in our case, poetry.

Neither of these perspectives is either philosophically credible – in the light of work by the likes of Michel Foucault – nor particularly applicable to an anthology of Persian poetry. The Iranian poet Nima Yushij's groundbreaking introduction of quasi-European *vers libre* techniques to Persian poetry in the early twentieth century, for example, may have instigated the beginning of *she're noe* – New Poetry – and other open forms that would eventually become the dominant style in Persian poetry; but neither Yushij's innovations nor his considerable influence could shorten the longevity of traditional closed forms such as the *ghazal* ode. At the time of writing this, arguably the most popular and internationally renowned living Persian-language poet, the Iranian Simin Behbahani, is indeed best known for her sophisticated, post-modernist *ghazalyaat*.

We have, nevertheless, felt compelled to divide the poems translated and collected for this anthology into the two general categories of classical and modern, to highlight at least one of the radical changes that have occurred in the theory and practice of Persian poetry, that is, a movement away from the popular classical verse forms such as the *ghazal*, *masnavi* (the heroic couplet) and *ruba'i* (the quatrain) towards open forms and the avant-garde.

One of our aims in emphasising this movement has been to show that, in opposition to imperialist / Orientalist views that perceive 'the East' as constant and unchangeable, the Middle Eastern poetics that we are presenting in this anthology is neither inherently hostile to change and experimentation nor in any need of an imposition of progressive Western aesthetics. At the same time, however, we hope to acknowledge that Western influence – as opposed to interference – did in fact play a crucial and constructive role towards the end of the nineteenth century by inspiring Persian intellectuals such as Yushij to inaugurate less rigid, more liberal discursive formations and, by doing so, to provide for an explosion of the hitherto suppressed voices, most notably those of Persian-speaking women poets.

If the advent of free verse, and its concomitant liberation of women poets, was one of the most significant events of the story of Persian poetry, the tale's first significant event was, to evoke a mythological trope, its creation.

Modern Persian – as distinct from Old and Middle Persians, the early Indo-European languages spoken by most subjects of the Sassanid Empire and written in a cuneiform script, prior to the Empire's sacking by Arab invaders in the seventh century CE – was created as an amalgam of Old / Middle Persian phonetics and grammar with a confluence of Arabic loanwords and the Arabic alphabet. This fusion – an outcome of temporary rule by, and an inevitable hybridisation with, a foreign culture – is perhaps similar to the production of Middle English as a consequence of the Francophone Normans' invasion.

The Arab Muslim conquest of the Sassanid Empire – which, at its height, had included almost all of the contemporary Middle East – did not only revolutionise the languages spoken and written by the region's various peoples, but also promoted the nascent religion of Islam to dominance in place of Zoroastrianism, the state religion of the Sassanid Empire. Therefore, by the time of the appearance of Modern, Arabised Persian in the poetry of Rudaki (often considered the first poet of Modern Persian and, therefore, the first poet appearing in this anthology) the language's speakers and writers, in spite of their different ethnic backgrounds (mostly Persian / Iranian, but also Turkic, Kurdish, Afghan and some Arabic), were almost all Muslims by religion and ruled by various Muslim sultans, caliphs and emirs.

It is at times unavoidable to view the term 'Persian' as anything other than synonymous, or at last coterminous, with 'Iranian'. This view is dubious for a number of reasons; for example, Iran, at least in a modern context, refers to a specific nation state within which a sizeable minority is neither ethnically nor linguistically Persian. Furthermore, many non-Iranians (e.g. the people of Afghanistan) also use forms of Persian language. In fact, some of the most illustrious figures of Persian poetry such as Rumi, Nezami, Mahasti and Jami were not ethnically Persian.

Yet, an association of Persian language with Iran / Iranian nation is also inescapable. The early Mediaeval Arabic conquest of regions once referred to as Mesopotamia, the Levant and, of course, the Arabian Peninsula, entailed a displacement of Middle Persian culture and language – and a near annihilation of the Zoroastrian religion – and the marginalisation and concentration of what remained of ancient Persian culture in a geographical region that correlates, more or less closely, with the territory of the modern state of Iran. Indeed, Modern Persian was in many ways the most strident, and perhaps most successful, expression of a desire for the revival of the pre-Islamic, non-Arabian civilisation which had nearly been erased by the Arab conquerors. As such, the advent of Modern Persian – and the work of early Modern Persian poets such as Rudaki and Ferdowsi – can be seen to have supported, or at least paralleled, an early Persian proto-nationalism that would, in due course, result in the establishment of a sovereign kingdom known to outsiders as Persia and to its own inhabitants as Iran.

The poems presented in the classical section of this anthology in some ways document the trials and traumas of the emergence and consolidation of the Persian / Iranian nation. The poet most closely associated with Persian patriotism, Ferdowsi, is also seen as the most committed poet of the Persian language – hence his being seen as a sort of early Iranian Dante – due to his composing the eleventh century epic poem *Shah-Nameh* (The Book of Kings) in a 'pure' Persian devoid of almost any Arabic loanwords.

As can be seen in the excerpts of Ferdowsi's work included in our anthology, Ferdowsi wrote – not unlike many other canonical epic poets – of arms, legendary military heroes and their righteous wrath. It was partly as a consequence of the seminal epic's resounding success – in rejuvenating both a subjugated people's language as well as their myths – that, for quite some time after Ferdowsi and perhaps well into the late-Middle Ages, the epic genre in general and rhyming couplets in particular remained the dominant form of Persian poetry as evidenced by, among other masterpieces of this period, Attar's *Mategh at-Tayr* (The Conference of the Birds), Nezami's *Leilee va Majnun* (Leila and Majnun), and Rumi's *Masnavi Ma'navi* (Spiritual Couplets), sometimes referred to as 'the Persian Quran', a designation which indicates the work's position as a mystical (Persian) rival to the religious

(Arabic) scripture.

If this strand of classical Persian poetry presented the nationalist / tribalist, or at any rate political, urges of the Persian-speakers of this era – most notably the ambitions of feudal (often Persianised Turkic) rulers who were in direct competition with the Arab caliphs – the much shorter form of the quatrain provided the poets with an outlet for voicing a witty, anti-authoritarian, and palpably anti-political discourse.

The quatrains of the twelfth century court entertainer Mahasti Ganjavi and those of her contemporary Omar Khayyam not only demonstrate a reluctance to participate in the discourses of national struggle and / or religious / sectarian conflict, but they altogether reject the macrocosmic concerns found in the epics, secular narrative poems and spiritual allegories. It is, perhaps not altogether surprisingly, this genre of classical Persian verse – with its illusive penchant for motifs such as wine drinking and sensual love – that has made the greatest impression on the Western imagination, culminating in the exotic image of the late-medieval genius Hafez as a drunkard and a hedonist whose poems, by conflating lay Sufi mysticism with the picaresque, put an end to the poetic hegemony of the epic and established Hafez's favoured form, the lyrical *ghazal*, as the dominant genre of Persian poetry for the next six centuries.

The triumph of Hafez, both as a poet and as a cultural icon, is instructive. By the time of the poet's rise to unprecedented levels of acclaim and popularity, both Arabic rulers and their local feudal rivals had been devastated by the ferocity of wave after wave of Asiatic invasions. The unimaginable brutality of Genghis Khan's assault in the thirteenth century and Tamerlane's in the fourteenth century left their marks on Persian literature: by, for example, forcing a young Rumi to flee his birthplace and contemplate separation and longing throughout his career as a Sufi scholar and poet; by fomenting Saadi's humanism as a response to the atrocities taking place around the poet; and by compelling Hafez to obscure the more risqué elements of his discourse in a pseudo-religious lexicon to evade the fury of the invaders. Hafez's ascendancy is also an expression of Modern Persian's maturity and confidence at the end of the Middle Ages, and the language's finding its most lucid and functional poetic register in the musicality and symbolism of the *ghazal*.

By the time Nima Yushij launched Persian free verse in the early twentieth century, however, Iran had reached a new nadir of cultural and societal decline. In the immediate aftermath of the Mongol invasions and the collapse of the Arabian caliphate, two competing empires had arisen in the Middle East – the Ottomans in the west and the Safavids in the east – and, in spite of incessant wars between the two powers, the presence of a central and unitary polity on either side prevented further cataclysmic foreign invasions and prompted something of a cultural and social revival contemporaneous with the European Renaissance.

The steep rise in Europe's navigational and martial capabilities, however, had a profoundly deleterious impact on the Middle Eastern empires. As a consequence of the merchants' growing dependency on the Western-dominated maritime routes, the land routes that connected Europe with the Far East, which had hitherto provided Iran and much of the Middle East with a great source of income, became redundant. Also, perhaps as a consequence of excessive, unsustainable agricultural activity, the previously arable lands became salinised and infertile, resulting in periodic crop failures and outbreaks of famine.

During the rule of the ineffective Qajar dynasty in the nineteenth century, what the Westerners had once referred to as the Persian Empire shrank in size under the blows of Russian expansionism in the north and the advances of the British Empire to Iran's east and south. As the Qajar shahs fell under the sway of the coercive agents of Western imperialism, food shortages and destitution ravaged the country, and religious fundamentalism took root as a result of the people's escalating dissatisfaction with their earthly conditions. Persian poets also suffered. One of the few truly gifted poets of this period, the mystic and proto-feminist activist Fatemeh, better known as Táhirih Qorrat al-Ayn, was executed due to her conversion to and preaching for an outlawed spiritual movement.

It was perhaps partly in response to the cruelty, intolerance and cultural atrophy during this period that the progressives and intellectuals, influenced by the Enlightenment and the democratic ideals of Europe, set about modernising Iran politically by introducing constitutional monarchy, and rejuvenating its literature by formulating free verse poetry. What follows is an account of Persian poetry from its conception in the early Middle Ages to its reinvention in the early twentieth century.

Ali Alizadeh

RUDAKI

Abdollah ibn-Mohammad Rudaki (858-941) is the first major poet of the modern Persian language. Although very little of his work survives – as collected in his *divan* (collected poems) after his death – he is often noted as the founder of classical Persian literature. He was born in what is now known as Tajikistan, where he is also buried.

from **DIVAN-E RUDAKI**

I will hold those ambergris-scented locks of yours
I will etch with kisses that jasmine leaf of yours

I will cast myself a thousand times in the dirt
Where you touch the earth with those feet of yours

I will plant a thousand kisses on your insignia
If I see a letter bearing that wax seal of yours

Command that Indian dagger to sever my hand
If I should one day caress that sleeve of yours

گرفت خواهم زلفین عنبرین ترا
به بوسه نقشکنم برگ یاسمین ترا

هر آن زمین که تو یک ره برو قدم بنهی
هزار سجده برم خاک آن زمین ترا

هزار بوسه دهم بر سخای نامهی تو
اگر ببینم بر مهر او نگین ترا

به تیغ هندی گو: دست من جدا بکنند
اگر بگیرم روزی من آستین تر

FERDOWSI

ABUL-GHASIM FERDOWSI OF TUS (935-1020) was born in what is now known as the Khorasan province of Iran. He began working on the *Shah-Nameh* (Book of Kings) in his early twenties and, according to tradition, spent the next thirty years of his life writing what would become Iran's national epic poem.

from the **SHAH-NAMEH**

Art is the sole realm of the Iranians
No other people possess the Terrible Lion

Iranians, united and spiritual
Are fearless before other people

I must learn about Iran's magnificence
Great is one who convenes with eminence

from the **SHAH-NAMEH**

What a catastrophe should Iran be ruined
If it becomes the den of lions and leopards

A place consumed by hardship and devastation
Where the dragon is enthroned with its sharp talons

An answer must be found now
So our hearts are relieved of sorrow

And only one who has been suckled by tigers
Can save us from these horrors

Rostam replies: This army and I
Have made a pact to fight with ferocity

If Kei Kaavoos so commands
I shall drive the Turks out of this land

هنر نزد ایرانیان است و بس
ندارند شیر ژیان را بکس

همه یکدلانند و یزدان شناس
به نیکی ندارند از کس هراس

مرا ارج ایران بباید شناخت
بزرگ انکه با نامداران بساخت

دریغ است ایران که ویران شود
کنام پلنگان و شیران شود

همه جای سختی و جای بلاست
نشستنگهه تیز چنگ اژدهاست

کنون چاره ای باید انداختن
دل خویش از رنج پرداختن

کسی کزپلنگان بخوردست شیر
ازین رنج ما را بود دسگیر

چنین داد پاسخ که من با سپاه
میان بسته ام جنگ را کینه خواه

چو یابم ز کاووس کی آگهی
کنام شهر ایران ز ترکان تهی

Let me lose my skin if Iran loses its skin
Let none survive in this land, this region

Better to be killed and beheaded slowly
Than to hand over our country to the enemy

Push aside comfort and indolence
Strive and embrace the suffering of flesh

As there's no gain without pain in this world
And one who is lazy will never find reward

There is renown to be found in bravery
Fortune has grown sick of the cowardly

If one hesitates even for a minute
His name will be forever dirt

It is better to be crushed under a stone
Than have my name shamed and forgotten

There is a story of a valiant leopard
Who battled with a fierce lion and said:

To spill my blood to make my name
Is better than life tormented by shame

There's no shame in dying courageously
And the death of the body makes for immortality

چو ایران نباشد تن من مباد
بدین بوم و بر زنده یک تن مباد

همه سر به سر تن به کشتن دهیم
از آن به که کشور به دشمن دهیم

تن آسانی و کاهلی دور کن
بکوش و زرنج تنت سورکن

که اندر جهان سود بی رنج نیست
کسی را که کاهل بود گنج نیست

در نام جستن دلیری بود
زمانه ز بد دل به سیری بود

اگر نیست ایدر فراوان درنگ
همان نام بهتر که ماند به ننگ

مرا سر نهان گر شود زیر سنگ
از آن به که نامم بر آید به ننگ

یکی داستان زد بر این بر پلنگ
چو با شیر جنگی در آمد به جنگ

بنام ار بریزی مرا گفت خون
به از زندگانی به ننگ اندرون

به نام نکو گر بمیرم رواست
مرا نام بهتر که تن مرگراست

OMAR KHAYYAM

OMAR IBN-IBRAHIM KHAYYAM OF NISHAPUR (1048-1122) was born in the province of Khorasan. Among the foremost scientists of his era, he worked as an astronomer and also contributed to the development of algebra. He also wrote numerous quatrains which were collected in *Rubaiyat-e Omar Khayyam* (The Quatrains of Omar Khayyam).

Three quatrains from the **RUBAIYAT**

1

Jamshid searched his Cup in that palace
Where deer now breed and the fox rests

Bahram, hunter of zebras all your life,
When the zebra hunted Bahram, did you notice?

2

Khayyam, if you've grown drunk on the cup, be cheerful
If you're sitting with a beauty whose face is the moon, be cheerful

Since the world is destined for annihilation
Imagine yourself already nil; be cheerful while you're still able.

3

Tipsy last night, I dropped by the tavern
I saw a drunken elder shouldering a jug of wine

Old man! I called. Aren't you humiliated before God?
God has mercy, he replied. Drink and don't whine!

۱

آن قصر که جمشید در او جام گرفت
آهو بچه کرد و روبه آرام گرفت

بهرام که گور میگرفتی همه عمر
دیدی که چگونه گور بهرام گرفت

۲

خیام اگر ز باده مستی خوش باش
با ماهرخی اگر نشستی خوش باش

چون عاقبت کار جهان نیستی است
انگار که نیستی چو هستی خوش باش

۳

سر مست بمیخانه کذر کردم دوش
پیری دیدم مست و سبوئی بر دوش

گفتم ز خدا شرم نداری ای پیر
گفتا کرم از خداست می نوش خموش

BABA TAHER

BABA TAHER (1000-1075?), also known as ORYAAN (the Naked) is recognised as one of the first poets of mystical love, later known as Sufism, in modern Persian. Very little is known about his life other than his being originally from the city of Hamadan, where he is also buried. He is best known for his lyrical *doe-bayt* (two verse) quatrains.

THREE QUATRAINS

1

From pain and medicine one makes a choice
From unity and separation one makes a choice

Out of medicine and pain and separation and unity
I look to what has been chosen by the loved one to make a choice

2

A howl comes from my heart, God! A howl is in my heart
No happiness has ever come from this heart

By tomorrow those who desire justice will desire shrieks
I will raise two hundred shrieks from my heart

3

The tree of misery has taken root in my being
At God's gate I am always moaning

Friends, enjoy each other's company
Humans are glass and death is unswerving

١

یکی درد و یکی درمان پسندد
یک وصل و یکی هجران پسندد

من از درمان و درد و وصل و هجران
پسندم آنچه را جانان پسندد

٢

خدایا داد از این دل داد از این دل
نگشتم یک زمان من شاد از این دل

چو فردا داد خواهان داد خواهند
بر آرم من دو صد فریاد از این دل

٣

درخت غم بجانم کرده ریشه
بدرگاه خدا نالم همیشه

رفیقان قدر یکدیگر بدانید
اجل سنگست و آدم مثل شیشه

MAHASTI

Maneejeh Ganjavi, known as Mahasti (1089-1159?), was born in the city of Ganja in what is now known as Azerbaijan. One of the earliest recorded female writers of the modern Persian language, she was a popular poet and performer at the court of the Seljuk monarch Sultan Sanjar. Although very little is known about her life, over two hundred of her *rubaiyat* (quatrains) remain.

FOUR QUATRAINS

1

Between houses of faith and perfidy is merely a breath
Between realms of doubt and certainty is merely a breath

This most precious breath must be savoured
As the fruit of our existence is merely a breath

2

It was sucking your ruby I ached for
It was swilling wine with you I ached for

In drunkenness and madness and sobriety
It was hearing your harp I ached for

3

Those nights I coyly slept with you are lost
Those gemstones I hung from my eyelashes are lost

You were the love of my life and a balm for my heart
You left and those secrets I shared with you are lost

۱

ازمنزل کفر تا به دین یک نفس است
وز عالم شک تا به یقین یک نفس است

این یک نفس عزیز را خوش می دار
کزحاصل عمرما همین یک نفست است

۲

لعل تو مکیدن آرزو می کردم
می با تو کشیدن آرزو می کردم

در مستی و در جنون و در هشیاری
چنگ تو شنیدن آرزو میکردم

۳

شبها که بنازبا توخفتم همه رفت
درها که به نوک مژده سفتم همه رفت

آرام دل و مونس جانم بودی
رفتم و هر آنچه با تو گفتم همه رفت

4

In one hand I hold a goblet and in the other the Quran
Sometimes the Permissible and sometimes the Forbidden

Beneath this unripe and raw dome
Neither absolute Infidel nor complete Muslim

۴

یک دست به مصفهیم و یک دست به جام
گه نزد حلالیم و گهی نزد حرام

ماییم در این گنبد ناپختیه خام
نه کافرمطلق نه مسلمان تمام

ATTAR

FARID OD-DIN ATTAR OF NISHAPUR (1124-1220?) lived in the city of Nishapur in what is now known as the Khorasan province of Iran. Although a drug maker and healer by profession, he made significant contributions to the incipient school of Persian mystical poetry. His most influential works include the *Mantegh at-Tayr* (The Conference of the Birds) and the *Asraar Nameh* (The Book of Secrets).

from the **MANTEGH AT-TAYR**

A wounded man was lamenting to a Sheikh
Why are you crying? asked the Sheikh

O Sheikh, I have lost my beloved
Whose face transformed my world

Her death killed me with sadness
The world blackened with loss

The Sheikh said: A heart made selfless
Will be your only recompense

Another love will be bestowed on you
Who, deathless, won't inflict sadness on you

A lover whose death brings loss
Is one whose love brings grief to life

A hundred afflictions will strike the face
Of whomever is struck by lust for a face.

دردمندي پيش شبلي ميگريـس
شيخ از او پرسيد كاين گريه ز چيست؟

گفت : شيخا دوسـتي بود آن مـن
كـز جمالـش تـازه بـودي جـان مـن

دي بـمـرد و مـن بـمـردم از غمـش
شـد جهـان بـر مـن سياه از ماتمش

شيخ گفتا شد دلت بيخويش از اين
خود نميباشد سـزايـت بـيـش از اين

دوسـتـي ديـگـر گـزيـن ايـن بـار تو
كــو نمـيـرد هـم نمـيـري زار تو

دوسـتـي كـز مـرگ نـقـصـان آورد
دوسـتـي او غـــم جـــان آورد

هـر كه شـد در عـشـق صورت مبتلا
هــم از آن صـورت فـتـد در صـد بـلا

from the **MATEGH AT-TAYR**

A Sheikh was asked by a dervish
Why Adam wandered from Paradise

The Sheikh said: When Adam, the blessed,
Stood before Heaven and bowed down his head

An absent voice rang out loudly
'This Place has trapped you in a hundred ways

Whoever in the realms beyond us
Bows down to things inferior to us

Will have all that is within annihilated
Or that person will never attain the Friend

A hundred thousand times over, be with the Beloved!
What is the value of a place devoid of the Beloved?

Those who are lit up by anything other than the Beloved,
Even if every one of them is Adam, will be cast aside...'

کرد شاگردی سال از اوستاد
کز بهشت آدم چرا بیرون فتاد

گفت بود آدم همی عالی گهر
چون به فردوسی فرو آورد سر

هاتفی برداشت آوازی بلند
کای بهشتت کرده از صد گونه بند

هرک در هر دو جهان بیرون ما
سر فروآرد به چیزی دون ما

ما زوال آریم بر وی هرچهست
زانک نتوان زد به غیر دوست دست

جای باشد پیش جانان صد هزار
جای بیجانان کجا آید به کار

هرک جز جانان به چیزی زنده شد
گر همه آدم بود افکنده شد

NEZAMI

NEZAM OD-DIN ABU MOHAMMAD NEZAMI-YE GANJAVI
(1141-1209) was born in the city of Ganja in what is
now known as Azerbaijan. Greatly influenced by
Ferdowsi's *Shah-Nameh*, Nezami produced a number
of immensely popular romantic narratives in the form
of *masnavi* (rhyming couplets), including *Khosrow o
Sheereen* (Khosrow and Shirin) and *Haft Peykar* (Seven
Figures).

from **HAFT PEYKAR**

That which is new as well as old
Is the word itself and the word within the word

Since the Creation no mother has birthed
A child more beneficial than the word

Never say that writers have died
When they have drowned in torrents of words

Since if you call the name of one you cherish
It will raise its head from the water like fish

Where is a word faultless like the spirit
Without which the treasury would remain a secret?

It knows the unheard stories
It reads the unwritten letters

See how of all that God created
Nothing remains of him beyond the word

If there's a testament left by 'mankind'
It is the word and the rest is the wind

From plants and minerals
To humans and animals

Try to search out that key to existence
Which remains until the world ends

Whoever comes to know who they are
Will lift high above life forever

آنچه او هم نوست و هم کهن است
سخن است و در این سخن سخن است

ز آفرینش نزاد مادر کن
هیچ فرزند خوبتر ز سخن

تا نگوئی سخنوران مردند
سر به آب سخن فرو بردند

چون بری نام هر کرا خواهی
سر برآرد ز آب چون ماهی

سخنی کو چو روح بیعیب است
خازن گنج خانه غیب است

قصه ناشنیده او داند
نامه نانبشته او خواند

بنگر از هرچه آفرید خدای
تا ازو جز سخن چه ماند به جای

یادگاری کز آدمیزاد است
سخن است آن دگر همه باد است

جهد کن کز نباتی و کانی
تا به عقلی و تا به حیوانی

باز دانی که در وجود آن چیست
کابدالدهر میتواند زیست

هر که خود را چنانکه بود شناخت
تا ابد سر به زندگی افراخت

SAADI

MOSLEH OD-DIN IBN-ABDOLLAH SAADI OF SHIRAZ (1200-1291?) lived in the city of Shiraz in what is now known as the province of Fars in Iran. After studying theology in Baghdad, he travelled across the Islamic world and collected oral narratives and anecdotes. He wrote his two masterpieces *Golestan* (The Rose Garden) and *Bustan* (The Orchard) after returning to his native city.

from the **GOLESTAN**

The tribe of Adam shares organs
From the same source of creation

If the times cause a particular organ distress
The other organs cannot hope for peace

You who stay cheerful despite others' pain
Perhaps don't deserve the name of "human"

Quatrain from **DIVAN-E SAADI**

Night after night goes by and I cannot close my eyes
I get drunk on thinking of you as everyone sleeps

If only you would kill me with your own hands
I could draw my last breath grasping your dress

بنی آدم اعضا ی یکدیگردند
که در آفرینش ز یک گوهرند

چو عضوی بدرد آورد روزگار
دگر عضوها را نماند قرار

تو کز محنت دیگران بی غمی
نشاید که نامت نهند آدمی

شبها گذرد که دیده نتوانم بست
مردم همه از خواب و من از فکر تو مست

باشد که به دست خویش خونم ریزی
تا جان بدهم دامن مقصود به دست

RUMI

Mowlana Jalal od-Din Mohammad Rumi (1207-1273?) was born in Balkh in what is now known as Afghanistan, and lived in Konya in what is now known as Turkey. He taught at the city's seminary until he became acquainted with the Sufi dervish Shams of Tabriz. This meeting resulted in his composition of the poems collected in the *Divan-e Shams-e Tabrizi* (Collected Poems for Shams of Tabriz) and the *Masnavi Ma'navi* (Spiritual Couplets).

Ghazal from **DIVAN-E SHAMS-E TABRIZI**

You will die, you must die from this Love, you must die
For you can absorb all that's above, if from this Love, you just die

You must die, you must not be afraid of this death,
You will grow from this soil and reach the heavens, you must die

You must die, you must die from this desire,
For this desire is like a rope that binds you, you must die

You must become an axe and defy and smash the prison
For you will become king and emir and the prison must die

You must die in the presence of the sweet emperor
For when you die in his presence you become regal, you must die

You must die, you must lift high above the cloud
For when you lift high above the cloud you are the exquisite
full moon, you must die

You must be silent, silence is a heartbeat from death
All life is held by those who have let their cacophony die

بمیرید بمیرید در این عشق بمیرید
در این عشق چو مردید همه روح پذیرید

بمیرید بمیرید و زین مرگ مترسید
کز این خاک برآیید سماوات بگیرید

بمیرید بمیرید و زین نفس بمیرید
که این نفس چو بندست و شما همچو اسیرید

یکی تیشه بگیرید پی حفره زندان
چو زندان بشکستید همه شاه و امیرید

بمیرید بمیرید به پیش شه زیبا
بر شاه چو مردید همه میر و وزیرید

بمیرید بمیرید و زین ابر برآیید
چو زین ابر برآیید همه بدر منیرید

خموشید خموشید خموشی دم مرگست
همه زندگی آنست که خاموش نفیرید

from the **MASNAVI MA'NAVI**

Listen to the reed weave its narration
Complain of all those separations

Since they cut me out from the marshes
Those who hear me moan are reduced to tears

I need a chest torn by separation
So that I can sing pain and passion

Whoever has been detached from their origins
Will eternally seek out union

I sighed in the company of all people
I befriended the joyful and the miserable

Each who befriended me out of their own acuity
Did not pursue the mysteries within me

My mystery is not far from my sigh
And yet it remains hidden from ear and eye

Soul is not hidden from body nor body from soul
Yet no one has been drawn to see the soul

بشنو از نی چون حکایت میکند
از جداییها شکایت میکند

کز نیستان تا مرا ببریده اند
در نفیرم مرد و زن نالیدهاند

سینه خواهم شرحه شرحه از فراق
تا بگویم شرح درد اشتیاق

هر کسی کو دور ماند از اصل خویش
باز جوید روزگار وصل خویش

من به هر جمعیتی نالان شدم
جفت بدحالان و خوشحالان شدم

هرکسی از ظن خود شد یار من
از درون من نجست اسرار من

سر من از نالهی من دور نیست
لیک چشم و گوش را آن نور نیست

تن ز جان و جان ز تن مستور نیست
لیک کس را دید جان دستور نیست

HAFEZ

Khawajeh Shams od-Din Mohammad Hafez of Shiraz (1320-1389?) lived in the city of Shiraz in what is now known as the Fars province of Iran. Although trained as a cleric, he left seminary and worked as a manual labourer, prior to becoming a court poet. His *ghazalyaat* (odes), as collected in the *Divan-e Hafez* (The Collected Poems of Hafez), incorporate the images of drinking songs and erotica with the motifs of Sufi mysticism.

Ghazal from **DIVAN-E HAFEZ**

The tomb of my friend, O dawn breeze, is where?
The home of that beautiful moon
                              so love-sickening and devious is where

The night is dark and the path to the safe valley stretches ahead
The place of vision is where, the mountain's blaze is where

All those who enter the world have a pattern to ruin
In the tavern for instance: the abstemious is where

The person who can divine knows how to be attentive
But there are many angles, keeper of secrets is where

Every strand of my hair has a thousand quibbles with you
What are we doing here, the idle one who accuses is where

Ask again for wave upon wave of her curls
His miserable and bewildered heart so tied in knots is where

Reason went insane, that black cascade is where
Heart retreated from us, the brow of the prize is where

Singer and wine-bringer and wine are prepared
Bliss cannot be prepared without a friend,
                              the friend of ours is where

Hafez, do not despair of autumn winds
                              rustling the grass of the world
Think it over logically, the thornless rose is where

ای نسیم سحر آرامگه یار کجاست
منزل آن مه عاشق کش عیار کجاست

شب تار است و ره وادی ایمن در پیش
آتش طور کجا موعد دیدار کجاست

هر که آمد به جهان نقش خرابی دارد
در خرابات بگویید که هشیار کجاست

آن کس است اهل بشارت که اشارت داند
نکتهها هست بسی محرم اسرار کجاست

هر سر موی مرا با تو هزاران کار است
ما کجاییم و ملامت گر بیکار کجاست

بازپرسید ز گیسوی شکن در شکنش
کاین دل غمزده سرگشته گرفتار کجاست

عقل دیوانه شد آن سلسله مشکین کو
دل ز ما گوشه گرفت ابروی دلدار کجاست

ساقی و مطرب و می جمله مهیاست ولی
عیش بی یار مهیا نشود یار کجاست

حافظ از باد خزان در چمن دهر مرنج
فکر معقول بفرما گل بی خار کجاست

Ghazal from **DIVAN-E HAFEZ**

Last night angels were at the tavern door and I saw them knocking
They took a cup and measured the clay of humanity they'd kneaded

Residents of the angels' harem, modest and veiled,
Took the drunkard's wine with me – the drifter – and drank

The sky could not hold the weight of their confidence
So my name, the madman's name, was chosen for the task

The seventy-two nations should be forgiven their wars
They couldn't see reality so it was legend they chased

I am grateful that between She and I peace has been made
The sylphs lifted their cups in gratitude and danced

Fire is not real if it only makes the candle smile
Fire is real when a pyre of moths is scorched

Only Hafez can so reveal the face of contemplation
Who takes his pen and combs the curls of speech

دوش دیدم که ملایک در میخانه زدند
گل آدم بسرشتند و به پیمانه زدند

ساکنان حرم ستر و عفاف ملکوت
با من راه نشین باده مستانه زدند

آسمان بار امانت نتوانست کشید
قرعه کار به نام من دیوانه زدند

جنگ هفتاد و دو ملت همه را عذر بنه
چون ندیدند حقیقت ره افسانه زدند

شکر ایزد که میان من و او صلح افتاد
حوریان رقص کنان ساغر شکرانه زدند

آتش آن نیست که از شعله او خندد شمع
آتش آن است که در خرمن پروانه زدند

کس چو حافظ نکشید از رخ اندیشه نقاب
تا سر زلف سخن را به قلم شانه زدند

JAMI

NUR OD-DIN ABDUL-RAHMAN JAMI (1414-1492) was born in what is now known as Afghanistan and was educated in the city of Herat. He became a Sufi and was one of the last prolific mystical poets of the Persian language. Among his works are the *Baharestan* (The Land of the Spring) and *Haft Awrang* (Seven Thrones).

from **HAFT AWRANG**

Qays received the party
Of visitors enthusiastically

They said among such and such a people
Lives a moon with the beauty of an angel

Layla is her name and she is desired
By countless suitors far and wide

The brilliance of her face is beyond adjectives
But go and see for yourself where she lives!

Don't expect the ear to act as the eye!
Seeing and hearing work differently

Upon hearing this story Qays rose
And adorned himself with new clothes

Roused by an inner passion, Ah… he gasped
He harnessed a camel and departed

He rode with a yearning for Layla
He rode until he reached the street of Layla

When Layla's people saw him near
They embraced him as one of theirs

They said that due to her unique goodness
She was placed high in the house

جمعی به دیار وی رسیدند
و آن میل و شعف ز وی بدیدند

گفتند که در فلان قبیله
ماهیست چو حور عین جمیله

لیلی آمد به نام و خیلی
هر سو به هواش کرده میلی

حسن رخش از صف برون است
هم خود برو و ببین که چون است

از گوش مجوی کار دیده
فرق است ز دیده تا شنیده

این قصه شنید قیس برخاست
خود را به لباس دیگر آراست

از شوق درون فغان برآورد
و آن ناقه به زیر ران درآورد

میراند در آرزوی لیلی
تا سر برود به کوی لیلی

چون مردم لیلیاش بدیدند
بر وی دم مردمی دمیدند

گفتند به نیکویی ثنایش
کردند به صدر خانه جایش

Yet though he searched for a glimpse of her
He detected no sign of his future

He lost hope and his heart faded
When suddenly he heard

The song of jewelry and jangle of an anklet
Transforming his mood with their music

And then saw a cypress so cherished
Swift as pheasant and warm as a partridge

With a face not made up to be rosy
Just for the sake of vanity yet still rosy

With eyes of a gazelle as though the gazelle
Had given her its eyes to make her beautiful

Every strand of her hair was a lariat
Wrapped around the feet of the heart

Layla and Qays were joyful to find each other
And set fire to each other's pyre

لیک از هر سو نظر همی تافت
از مقصد خود اثر نمی‌یافت

خون گشت ز ناامیدیاش دل
ناگاه برآمد از مقابل

آواز حلی و بانگ خلخال
گرداند سماع آن بر او حال

در حلهی ناز دید سروی
چون کبک دری روانتذروی

رویی ز حساب وصف بیرون
گلگونه نکرده لیک گلگون

آهو چشمی که گویی آهو
چشمش به نظاره دوخت بر رو

هر موی ز زلف او کمندی
بر پای دلی نهاده بندی

گشتند به روی یکدگر خوش
در خرمن هم زدند آتش

VAHSHI BAFQI

VAHSHI BAFQI (1532-1583) was born in the central province of Yazd. He worked as a schoolteacher in the city of Kashan prior to his poetry gaining popularity. He became panegyrist to the local ruler before dying of excessive drinking in Yazd.

GHAZAL

When we cut ourselves short, we cut ourselves short
When we abandon hope, we abandon it

The heart is not a pigeon that would land after taking off
When we leap from the corner of the roof, we leap from it

It was always a mistake to drive the prey from yourself
Now that you've driven us away, you've driven us from it

We imagined seeing your garden of Eden
We didn't see your paradise, we didn't see it

The glory of spring flowers is through a hundred gardens
                                        and the orchard
We didn't pick the fruit of any garden, we didn't pick it

The blade of devotion runs through us from head to foot
                                        and you are blind
Grow aware of our devotion for when we offer it, we offer it

The cause of Vahshi's seclusion and manner of speech
Is not something we've missed, we haven't missed it

ما چون ز دری پای کشیدیم کشیدیم
امید ز هر کس که بریدیم بریدیم

دل نیست کبوتر که چو برخاست نشیند
از گوشه بامی که پریدیم پریدیم

رم دادن صید خود از آغاز غلط بود
حالا که رماندی و رمیدیم رمیدیم

کوی توکه باغ ارم و روضهی خلد است
انگار که دیدیم ندیدیم ندیدیم

صد باغ بهار است و صلای گل و گلشن
گر میوهی یک باغ نچیدیم نچیدیم

سرتا به قدم تیغ دعاییم و تو غافل
هان واقف دم باش رسیدیم رسیدیم

وحشی سبب دوری و این قسم سخنها
آن نیست که ما هم نشنیدیم شنیدیم

HATEF ESFEHANI

HATEF ESFEHANI (?-1783) was born in Isfahan in central Iran, and studied philosophy, mathematics and foreign languages. He was best known for his mystical *ghazalyaat* (odes) which were compiled after his death in *Divan-e Hatef-e Esfehani* (The Collected Poems of Hatef Esfehani).

GHAZAL

What a night when you call me secretly to your
                                            bedroom's intimacy
You have me sit beside you and you sit beside me

Don't drive me from your door when I am old and broken
Because I have squandered my youth grieving over you,
                                            O young one

I am distraught and weep for one who has recently left
                                            on an expedition
May you reach your destination if you will have me reach mine

به حریم خلوت خود شبی چه شود نهفته بخوانیم
بنکار من بنشینی و بنکار خود بنشانیم

من اگر پیرم و ناتوان تو از آستان خودم مران
که گذشته در غمت ایجوان همه روزگار جوانیم

منم ای برید و دو چشم تر ز فراق آنه نو سفر
بمراد خود برسی اگر بمراد خود برسانیم

TÁHIRIH QORRAT AL-AYN

TÁHIRIH QORRAT AL-AYN (1817-1852) was a proto-feminist theologian and a priestess of the Bábí faith. She studied at a number of important seminaries in Iraq before returning to Iran to proselytise for the outlawed faith. She was arrested by the Qajar regime's police and executed in Tehran.

GHAZAL

If my gaze should ever chance upon you, come face to face,
I shall tell how sad you've made me, moment by moment,
$\qquad$ piece by piece

In the course of seeing your face, I've wafted like a breeze
Stranded valley to valley, street to street, house to house

The heart's blood flows from my eyes because of your absence
From spring to spring, stream to stream, river to river, seas to seas

Surrounding your delicate mouth, the perfumed design
$\qquad$ of your face,
Flower upon flower, bud upon bud, tulip on tulip,
$\qquad$ incense upon incense

Your eyebrows and eyes and beauty-spot have ensnared
$\qquad$ the bird of the heart
Desire by desire, spirit to spirit, love upon love, heart to heart

The sombre heart has woven your love into life's carpet
Thread upon thread, warp to warp, weft to weft,
$\qquad$ filament to filament

Táhirih examined her heart and found nothing but you there
From page to page, core to core, drape to drape, centre to centre

گر بتو افتدم نظر چهره به چهره رو به رو
شرح دهم غم ترا نکته به نکته مو بمو

از پی دیدن رخت همچو صبا فتاده ام
خانه به خانه در به در کوچه به کوچه کو به کو

میرود از فراق تو خون دل از دو دیده ام
دجله به دجله یم به یم چشمه به چشمه خون به خون

دور دهان تنگ تو عارض عنبرین خطت
غنچه به غنچه گل به گل لاله به لاله بو به بو

ابرو و چشم و خال تو صیدنموده مرغ دل
طبع به طبع و دل به دل مهر به مهر و خون به خون

مهر ترا دل حزین بافته بر قماش جان
رشته به رشته نخ به نخ تاربه تار و پو به پو

در دل خویش طاهره گشت و ندید جز ترا
صفحه به صفحه لا به لا پرده به پرده تو به تو

II
MODERN PERSIAN VERSE

The twentieth century has been, to quote the historian Eric Hobsbawm, an 'age of extremes'. The monumental movements that shook, demolished and in turn aggressively revived many tenets of 'Old Persia' during the last century have been nothing short of extreme, both in their volatile theories and in their violent applications.

The Constitutional Revolution of 1906 unified the progressive middle class intellectuals with radical members of the clergy to oust the despised Qajar dynasty. The accession to the throne of Reza Shah Pahlavi in 1925 ushered in an era of dictatorial reforms which antagonised the religious whilst making great advances in modernising the society and promoting women's rights. The 1953 CIA-engineered *coup d'état* toppled the government of the democratically elected prime minister Mosaddegh and established Mohammad-Reza, the son of the previous Pahlavi shah, as Iran's absolute monarch. The 1979 Islamic Revolution smashed the Pahlavi dynasty, replacing it with a puritanical, theocratic republic led by a censorious 'Supreme Leader'. The brutal Iran-Iraq war in the immediate aftermath of the Islamic Revolution cost close to one million lives; and the hostility between the intransigent rulers of the Islamic Republic and the United States of America, Gulf Arab kingdoms and Israel continues to be the source of regional dread and international anxiety. As with most other Middle Eastern countries, Iran's story in the twentieth century has been characterised by war, devastating political turmoil and seemingly intractable contestations and conflicts.

Iranian poets' work over the last hundred years has registered, opposed and at times legitimised Iran's tumults and crises. The poets included in the second section of our anthology have been, and continue to be, active participants in the unfolding drama of their people's precarious struggle to, on the one hand, approach and embrace modernity and a level of material stability while, on the other hand, fend off (real and perceived) foreign threats while accommodating a more or less steadfast fidelity to their Islamo-Persian cultural identity.

As mentioned in the introduction to this anthology's first section, Nima Yushij's break with formal conventions of classical Persian versification was a clear attempt at rejecting the outdated values associated with the country's socio-political decline in the nineteenth century. At the same time, however, many of Yushij's free verse disciples such as Mehdi Akhavan-Sales and Ahmad Shamlu retained much of the symbolism, mythological references and archaic vocabulary of classical Persian poetry. Even among today's poets of the Persian diasporas in the West, the classical is far from forgotten. The poem 'Ghazal, after Hafez' by Mimi Khalvati, not only evokes the language and imagery of Hafez's poetry but also imitates the form of the mediaeval master's *ghazalyaat*. (Khalvati's poem, as well as the piece by another diaspora poet, Sholeh Wolpé, are originally written in English and therefore not translated by the editors of this anthology.)

While it can be said that most Persian poets of the modern and post-modern milieus were and continue to be preoccupied with balancing their desires for progress with their attachment to a specific sense of ethnic identity, there can be no denying that something genuinely new did take place during the development of Persian poetry in the twentieth century. The mid-century poetry of the young woman writer and filmmaker Forough Farrokhzad, for example, was absolutely revolutionary in its rejection of the ornate lyricism and highbrow artificiality of earlier (male-dominated) Persian poetry.

Farrokhzad's poems, which proved crucial in stirring and launching the work of the future generations of Iranian women poets, were written in an unpretentious, prosaic voice and articulated seemingly mundane themes such as, in the case of her poem 'The Bird, Only a Bird', the banality and boredom of life in a modern city. By carefully mimicking everyday speech and refusing to adapt a self-consciously poetic diction, Farrokhzad's poetry transcended conventional realism and was seen as a form of linguistic resistance against the hegemony of both the classicists and the feted modernists. Farrokhzad's influence was felt, and continues to be felt, in work by Persian women poets, from Tahereh Saffarzadeh to Bahareh Rezai, who also reject both the rigidity of classical verse and the apparent obscurantism of excessively experimental modernist poetry.

Another significant development of Iranian poetry in the twentieth century has been the manifestation of the political and / or revolutionary politics in the work of traditionalist as well as modernist poets. Whilst one can detect a simulation of the dramas unfolding in the Persia of the Middle Ages in the cryptic symbols and allusions of, for example, Ferdowsi's *Shah-Nameh* or the quatrains of Omar Khayyam, direct depictions of not only modern Iran's political scenes / disruptions as well as the poets' own – often radical – political volitions are found in abundance in the poems presented in this section of our anthology.

Parvin Etesami's early twentieth century 'The Tear of an Orphan', for example, may have the form of a classical *ghazal*, but its declaration of the poet's contempt for her society's predatory rulers and greedy clergy is absolutely explicit and, in the context of the continuum of Persian poetry, an unmistakable expression of the new, politically committed voice of poets in general and woman poets in particular. Partow Nooriala's 'Woman', written towards the end of the century, is equally unflinching in its depiction and denunciation of the ghastly treatment of many women – particularly the working class women deemed immoral – in contemporary Iranian society.

If new developments such as free verse, feminist perspectives and political engagement distinguish modern and contemporary Persian poetry from the poetry presented in the first section of this anthology, there also exists much rapport between the classical and the modern in the poetry included in this volume. There is, for example, something palpably mystical and esoteric about Shamlu's 'The Journey', bringing to mind the Sufism of mediaeval poets such as Attar. The youngest and final author presented in our anthology, the 'Generation Y' poet Ahmad Zahedi Langroodi, may be seen as a representative of today's technology savvy writers – his work having won Iran's first Internet poetry prize in 2002 – but his poem 'Thread of the Noose' resonates with the melancholy tone of the reed flute in Rumi's thirteenth century *masnavi*.

A final note must be made regarding our inclusion of poems written by Iranian and (in the case of the diaspora poets) Iranian-born poets in this section of our anthology. In the previous section we included Persian poets who, according to a contemporary designation of national identities, cannot be considered Iranian. Rumi, for example, would be considered either a citizen of Afghanistan or of Turkey if he was born today, and Nezami could be seen as an Azerbaijani. As mentioned before, this decision was in keeping with the commonly held view that during the Middle Ages, Persian was widely used – particularly for literary purposes – beyond the boundaries of contemporary Iran.

Our decision to include only poets who can be considered as Iranian or Iranian-born in this, modern section of our anthology, on the other hand, has been made in recognition of the fact that, during the twentieth century, Persian was almost entirely and systematically eradicated in many modern nation states other than Iran; and that Iran became the centre of Persian literary activity. Our selection should not be seen as a chauvinistic / exclusionary gesture, but one necessitated by an understanding of the modern – and disputatious – connections between linguistic and national identities. Our decision not to include contemporary Afghan and Tajik poets who write in Dari Persian or Tajik Persian, for example, was made neither to imply that the Persians spoken in Afghanistan and Tajikistan are not 'real' Persian, nor to deny the merits and significance of work by non-Iranian Persian-language writers. This decision was made to avoid any unintended suggestions *vis-à-vis* the cultural and political sovereignty of Afghanistan, Tajikistan and / or the ideology of Iranian expansionism.

We will not deny, however, that today Persian poetry crosses boundaries and national / ethnic divides as it did during the Middle Ages. The fact that a number of poets who identify themselves as Persian and have Persian as their first language, write poetry in languages other than Persian (e.g. English in the case of the two diaspora poets included in this volume) demonstrates the nomadic movement of a linguistically specific poetics across linguistic divides.

This very anthology, and the existence of many recent volumes that attempt similar things in different cross-cultural contexts, is a testimony to the transportability and flexibility of poetry and the art-form's ability, finally, to transcend rigid ethno-cultural divisions to emphasise what the thinker Walter Benjamin has referred to as the 'kinship of languages'.

In a world beset by the vulgar appearances of ethnic separatism, religious intolerance and all manners of tribalism – perhaps precipitated by the misguided, disingenuous and devastating utopianism of 'globalisation' to impose a free market 'global village' across the world – one can hope it is an appreciation of poetic and linguistic kinship, as opposed to in/tolerance of cultural differences, that is achieved by this, our anthology of Persian poetry in English.

Ali Alizadeh

NIMA YUSHIJ

NIMA YUSHIJ (1896-1959) was the founder of Persian free verse or 'New Poetry'. Although initially ignored by the literary establishment, the bulk of his poems appeared gradually in literary journals and anthologies during the 1920s and 1930s. His break with traditional Persian versification was influenced by the French Symbolists.

THE PHOENIX

The world-famous phoenix, sonorous bird,
impoverished by the squall of bitter winds
perches solitary
on a protruding branch.
She is surrounded by birds on every branch.

She mingles remote cries
from shreds of hundreds of distant voices
like a dark horizon above the mountain in clouds
she constructs
the wall of an imaginary building.
From the moment when the sun's yellowness
pales on waves building to a crescendo on the beach
the howl of a jackal, and a villager
kindling fire in a secret place.
Red-eyed, the young flame
defines night's large pair of eyes
and in isolated places
people are moving.
With that extraordinary song so utterly hidden
she leaps from the branch where she has rested.
Through light and darkness of endless night
among the things that become entangled
she passes.
She stares at the flame
before her.

A place without flowers, breathless.
Stubborn sunlight bursts over rocks,

ققنوس

ققنوس، مرغ خوشخوان، آوازه ی جهان،
آواره مانده از وزش بادهای سرد،
برشاخ خیزران،
بنشسته است فرد
برگرد او به هر سر شاخی پرندگان

او ناله های گمشده ترکیب میکند،
از رشته های پیره ی صدها صدای دور،
در ابرهای مثل خطی تیره روی کوه،
دیوار یک بنای خیالی
میسازد.
از آن زمانی که زرد ی خورشید روی موج
کمرنگ مانده است و به ساحل گرفته اوج
بانگ شغال، و مرد دهاتی
کرده ست روشن آتش پنهان خانه را.
قرمز به چشم، شعله ی خردی
خط می کشد به زیر دو چشم درشت شب
واندر نقاط دور،
خلقند در عبور.
او، آن نوای نادره، پنهان چنان که هست،
از آن مکان که جای گزیده ست میپرد.
در این چیزها که گره خورده میشود
با روشنی و تیرگی این شب دراز
می گذرد
یک شعله را به پیش
می نگرد.

جایی که نه گیاه در آنجاست، نه دمی،
ترکیده آفتاب سمج روی سنگهاش،

she feels the desires of her kind
dark as fumes and neither earth nor its life
are enticing. Their hopes
appear like stacks of burning wood
to pale morning's eye.
She perceives that whereas other birds
are content
with eating and sleeping
her life is torment beyond description.

Magnificent singing bird
in the place of veneration by fire,
place now transformed into an inferno,
has withdrawn her tail plumes, her piercing eyes
trembling.
And suddenly, on the mountain,
as she flails her feathers and wings,
intoxicated by intimate torment
a scream bursts from the bottom of a bitter, burning heart
with a meaning hidden from any passing bird
and she hurls herself into the majestic flames.
An intense wind blows and the bird is incinerated!
The phoenix has configured the ashes of her body!
Her chicks emerge from the heart of the ashes.

نه این زمین و زندگی اش چیز دلکش است
حس میکند که آرزو ی مرغها چو او
تیره ست همچو دود.اگر چند امیدشان
چون خرمنی ز آتش
در چشم مینماید و صبح سفیدشان.
حس میکند که زندگی او چنان
مرغان دیگر ار بسر آید
در خواب و خورد،
رنجی بود کز آن نتوانند نام برد.

آن مرغ نغز خوان،
در آن مکان ز آتش تجلیل یافته،
اکنون، به یک جهنم تبدیل یافته،
بسته ست دمبدم نظر و میدهد تکان
چشمان تیزبین.
وز روی تپه،
ناگاه، چون به جای پر و بال میزند
بانگی بر آراد از ته دل سوزناک و تلخ،
که معنیش نداند هر مرغ رهگذر
آنگه ز رنجهای درونش مست،
خود را به روی هیبت آتش می افکند.
باد شدید میدمد و سوخته ست مرغ!
خاکستر تنش را اندوخته ست مرغ!
پس جوجه هاش از دل خاکسترش به در.

PARVIN ETESAMI

Parvin Etesami (1906–1941) was born in Tabriz and began her career by publishing poetry in her father's literary magazine. She soon became a hugely successful poet thanks to her series of short poems, *Mast vali hoshyar* (Drunk Yet Aware). She died of typhoid fever and was buried in Qom.

THE TEAR OF AN ORPHAN

Once upon a time a king travelled a highway
Cries of exaltation rose from every roof and valley
From amidst the clamour an orphaned child asked
What's that on the king's crown that's so shiny?
Someone answered: How could I know?
It certainly seems to be an object of great luxury
An old hunchback woman drew near and said:
That is the blood of your heart and the tear of my eye
We have been hoodwinked by the shepherd's crook and cloak
This wolf has been using on his flock continually
The priest is a thief when he procures property and a village
The king is a beggar when he devours his subject's property
Consider the single tear-drop of an orphan
To understand why that jewel in the crown is so shiny
Parvin, what's the point of speaking truthfully to the deluded?
What kind of person wants to hear words of reality?

اشك یتیم

روزی گذشت پادشهی از گذرگهی
فریاد شوق بر سر هر کوی و بام خاست

پرسید زان میانه یکی کودک یتیم
کاین تابناک چیست که بر تاج پادشاست

آن یک جواب داد چه دانیم ما که چیست
پیداست آنقدر که متاعی گرانبهاست

نزدیک رفت پیرزنی کوژپشت و گفت
این اشک دیدهی من و خون دل شماست

ما را به رخت و چوب شبانی فریفته است
این گرگ سالهاست که با گله آشناست

آن پارسا که ده خرد و ملک، رهزن است
آن پادشا که مال رعیت خورد گداست

بر قطرهی سرشک یتیمان نظاره کن
تا بنگری که روشنی گوهر از کجاست

پروین، به کجروان سخن از راستی چه سود
کو آنچنان کسی که نرنجد ز حرف راست؟

SHAHRIAR

Seyyed Mohammad Hossein Tabrizi, known as Shahriar (1906-1988), was born in Tabriz, in Iranian Azerbaijan, and published his first collection of poetry at 23. Among his works is *Heydar babaaye salaam* (Greetings to Baba Heydar), written in Azeri Turkish.

from **ALAS, MY MOTHER**

1

Thinking of soup and vegetables for her sick ones
She slowly passed the stairs
Though a black halo hovered above her
She is dead though continues to nurse us
She can be sensed everywhere in our lives
Every corner of the house holds a scene from her story
She arranged her own funeral
My poor mother

2

Every day she passed beneath these stairs
Quietly so she wouldn't disturb my beauty sleep
She passed by again today
Opening and closing the door
She moves with a hunched back through alleyways
She has wrapped her head in a pepper-black prayer veil
Wrinkled shoes and darned socks
She is thinking about the children
No matter what happens she must buy carrots today
Poor old woman; the alleyways are buried beneath snow.

6

No, she isn't dead; I can hear her voice
She is struggling with the children
'Nahid! Be quiet!

ای وای مادرم

۱

آهسته باز از بغل پله ها گذشت
در فکر آش و سبزی بیمار خویش بود
امّا گرفته دور و برش هاله ای سیاه
او مرده است و باز پرستار حال ماست
در زندگی ما همه جا وول می خورد
هر کُنج خانه صحنه ای از داستان اوست
در ختم خویش هم به سر کار خویش بود
بیچاره مادرم

۲

هر روز می گذشت از این زیر پله ها
آهسته تا بهم نزند خواب ناز ما.
امروز هم گذشت
در باز و بسته شد
با پشت خم از این بغل کوچه می رود
چادر نماز فلفلی انداخته به سر
کفش چروک خورده و جوراب وصله دار
او فکر بچه هاست
هر جا شده هویج هم امروز می خرد
بیچاره پیرزن، همه برف است کوچه ها.

۶

نه، او نمرده، میشنوم من صدای او
با بچه ها هنوز سر و کله میزند
ناهید، لال شو

Bijan, stand over there
Show me your hands, no noise!'
She was making soup for her sick ones.

7

She died and was buried next to father
Her relatives came to pay their respects
The funeral service was okay.
We received many condolences.
Thanks for your concern.
But my heart kept saying:
These words will not be a mother to you.

8

Who was it
Pulled the discarded quilt up over me last night
Shifted the glass of water?
At midnight
A ghastly dream and I woke suddenly, feverish.
Just before dawn
She was again sitting here at my feet
Gently praying
No, she's not dead.

بیژن، برو کنار
کفگیر بی صدا
دارد برای نا خوش خود آش میپزد.

٧

او مرد ودر کنار پدر زیر خاک رفت
اقوامش آمدند پی سر سلامتی
یک ختم هم گرفته شد و پر بدک نبود.
بسیار تسلیت که به ما عرضه داشتند.
لطف شما زیاد
اما ندای قلب بگوشم همیشه گفت:
این حرفها برای تو مادرنمیشود.

٨

پس این کی بود؟
دیشب لحاف رد شده بر روی من کشید
لیوان آب از بغل من کنار زد،
در نصفه های شب
یک خواب سهمناک و پریدم به حال تب.
نزدیکهای صبح
او باز زیر پای من اینجا نشسته بود
آهسته با خدا،
راز و نیاز دشت
نه، او نمرده است.

9

No, she's not dead because I am alive
She's alive in my sorrow, poetry, imagination
Whatever tradition of poetry I have I have from her
Could the hearth of the sun or the moon ever be switched off?
Could that lioness die? She gave birth to shah-riar
Her heart is rejuvenated by love and can never die.

16

Don't ask what state I was in when I got home
There she was, as usual, sitting next to the fishpond
She had laundered my dirty shirt again
She seemed to be laughing although she was disconsolate:
'So off you went and buried me then came home, eh?
I will never abandon you, o wretched boy.'
I wanted to laugh out loud at her mistake
But it was a hallucination
Alas, my mother.

۹

نه او نمرده است که من زنده ام هنوز
او زنده است در غم و شعرو خیال من
میراث شاعرانه ی من هر چه هست از اوست
کانون مهر و ماه مگر میشود خموش؟
آن شیر زن نمیرد؟ او شهریار زاد
هرگز نمیرد آنکه دلش زنده شد به عشق.

۱۶

باز آمدم به خانه چه حالی! نگفتنی
دیدم نشسته، مثل همیشه، کنار حوض
پیراهن پلید مرا باز نشسته بود
انگار خنده کرد ولی دلشکسته بود:
"بردی مرا به خاک سپرده و آمدی؟
تنها نمی گذارمت ای بینوا پسر."
میخواستم به خنده درآیم ز اشتباه
اما خیال بود
ای وای مادرم.

AHMAD SHAMLU

Aʜᴍᴀᴅ Sʜᴀᴍʟᴜ (1925-2000) was a poet, children's writer and journalist. One of the most important purveyors of modernist free verse in Iran, his volumes of poetry include *Havaaye taaze* (Fresh Air), *Ghoghnoos dar baaran* (The Phoenix in the Rain), and *Ibraahim dar aatash* (Abraham in Flames).

THE JOURNEY

On a red evening they arrived
out of the furnaces of the east, two girls, next to me.
Tanned and ragged, copper-cheeked,
Venus danced in the depthless night of their eyes,
compelling them westwards.
They said to me:
' – Head west with us!'

But I kept reading
and remained silent
and read away the entire night
and warmed the entire hollow darkness with my song.

On a damp morning they arrived
on the roads from the north, two girls, next to me.
Their lips were wild and cracked
like the stone of a peach
and their thighs
were the marble of Hindu temples
and they said to me:
' – Travel with us!'
Yet I
suppressed in my mouth the song I had been weaving from
horizon to horizon
and cast the weight of my silent eyes upon their turbulent eyes
and remained quiet for half a day
under the rain of the sun's rays, I passed half the day in silence.

سفر

در قرمز غروب رسیدند
از کوره راه شرق، دو دختر، کنار من.
تابیده بود و تفته، مس گونه هایشان
ورقص زهره که در گود بی ته شب چشمشان بود
به دیارغرب
ره آورد شان بود.
و با من گفتند:
با ما بیا به غرب!

من اما همچنان خواندم
و جوابی بدانان ندادم
و تمام شب را خواندم
تمام خالی تاریک شب را از سرودی گرم آکندم

در ژاله بارصبح رسیدند
از جاده ی شمال، دودختر، کنار من.
لبهایشان چو هسته ی شفتالو
وحشی و پرترک بود
و ساقهایشان
با مرمر معابد هندو
می مانست
و با من گفتند:
با ما بیا با راه!
ولیکن من
لب فرو بستم ز آوازی که می پیچیدم ازآفاق تا آفاق
و بر چشمان غوغا شان نهادم ثقل چشمان سکوتم را
و نیم روز را خاموش ماند
به زیر بارش پر شعله ی خورشید، نیمی از گذشت روز را خاموش ماندم.

Out of the heart of midday
a group of men arrived from the furnaces of the west...
Reflected in their eyes
and jaws, stern
like rocks covered in algae,
was the sun of searching and questing.

They examined me in great silence.
I rose from my spot, set my foot to the road, and my anthem staged
our march to its steady beat.

On a deserted spot, my memory stood
vague and silenced
and did not cry after me.
And as soon as our shadows and my anthem
vanished on the misty road,
out of desertion and loneliness
in the night's gloomy solitude   it cried.

در قلب نیمروز
از کوره راه غرب رسیدند چند مرد...
خورشید جست و جو
در چشمهایشان متلالی بود
و فکشان، عبوس
با صخرهها ی پور خزه می مانست.

در ساکت بزرگ به من دوخته چشم.
برخاستم ز جای، نهادم به راه پای، و در راه دوردست سرودم شماره زاد
با ضربها ی پر تبشش گامهایمان را.

بر جای لیک، خاطره ام گنگ
خاموش ایستاد
دنبال ما نگریست.
و چندان که سایه مان و سرود من
در راه پرغبار نهان شد،
در خلوت عبوس شبانگاه
بر ماندگی و بی کس خوشین   گریست.

FEREYDOON MOSHIRI

FEREYDOON MOSHIRI (1926-2000) was born in Tehran, and his first book was published when he was 29. Among his collections are *Gonaahe daryaa* (The Ocean's Guilt), *Abr va koocheh* (The Cloud and the Alley) and *Lahzeha va ehsaas* (Moments and Sensation).

THE NIGHTS OF KARUN

Dark nights
stifling nights
hushed nights.

Nights beneath the umbrella of grief
                                    other nights
nights of prison
nights of shackles
nights without the lamp of moonlight
nights of swamps
cold nights of falling leaves
nights of pain for those escaping themselves
nights behind the ninth curtain of darkness
nights of estrangement
nights of driving isolation, without a shred of light
nights of compulsion
nights of fear of death
                                    nights of wakefulness
nights of the scream.

Nights like the howl of thunder, roar of bullets
each time life is torn apart with a nocturnal screech
nights when fury rages upon doors and roofs
nights of delirium
nights when the galaxies' trajectory
                                    is reddened
                                    by the pyramid of fire.

شبهای کارون

شبهای تاریک
شبهای دلتنگ
شبهای خاموش.

شبهای زیر چت غم
شبهای دیگر

شبهای زندان
شبهای زنجیر
شبهای بی فانوس مهتاب
شبهای مرداب
شبهای سرد برگ ریزان
شبهای دارد مردمی در خود گریزان
شبهای پشت پرده ی نه توی ظلمت
شبهای غربت
شبهای کنج انزوا، بی ذره ای نور
شبهای مجبور
شبهای مرگ زندگی
شبهای بیدار

شبهای فریاد.

شبها که چون آوای تندر، نعره ی تیر
جان می شکافد هر زمان تا بانگ شبگیر
شبها که وحشت می خروشد بر در و بام
شبهای سرسام
شبها که راه کهکشان
از هرم آتش
سرخ رنگ است.

Nights of war!
Nights when the ground quakes, hundreds of times an instant
nights when children's hearts stop still
nights of torrential rain
nights of electricity from a torch, gunpowder smoke
opening a path to the star's elevation
nights of blood-soaked barricades
nights of shredded flesh
nights when across the span of the Karun
nothing is what it seems

                          that: mouth full of blood.

Sad nights
nights when many innocents
fall like leaves upon the dirt
nights of bitter loyalty
nights of thick black mourning
nights when the strength of expectant mothers
entwines spirit with sorrow
and becomes a shattered voice, a shriek
'Oh God', and lamentation
nights of shock
nights of regret
in the narrow corridor of darkest darkness
life is kept alive by the hope that tomorrow
– a tomorrow almost here –
this silenced nation
will let out a roar of liberty on the morning of victory
and grow wings in the glittering paradise.

شبها که جنگ است!
شبها که می لرزد زمین، هر لحظه صد بار
شبها که قلب کودکان می افتد از کار،
شبهای رگبار
شبها که برق شعله افکن، دود باروت
ره می گشاید تا بلندای ستاره
شبهای سنگرهای خونین
شبهای پیکرهای پاره
شبها که در پهنای بی آرام کارون
دیگر نه آن است این
که: لب پر می زند خون

شبهای غمناک
شبها که خیل بیگناهان
چون برگ می افتند بر خاک
شبهای تلخ بردباری
شبهای سنگین و سیاه سوگواری
شبها که قوت مادران چشم بر در
با روح مالامال اندوه
بغض است و فریاد
وای است و زاری
شبهای حیرت
شبهای حسرت
در تنگنایی اینچنین تاریک تاریک
جان را امیدی زنده می دارد که فردا
- فردای نزدیک -
این خلق خاموش
با صبح پیروزی کشد بانگ رهایی
پر می گشاید در بهشت روشنایی

SIMIN BEHBAHANI

SIMIN BEHBAHANI (b. 1927) is one of Iran's most respected living poets, and was considered a nominee for the 1997 Nobel Prize in Literature. Her collections include *Jaay-e paa* (Footprint), *Marmar* (Marble), and *Chelcheraagh* (Chandelier).

YOU SAID IT'S A GRAPE

You said: "It's a grape." I said: "That's not clear."
You insisted: "Believe me! Every year
I harvest a branch. This is the garden of history,
We pick the few grapes these vines bear…"

Your hand moved; you were plucking grapes…
I said: "My religion has no place for humour."
You said: "Close your eyes, open your mouth
So that I can quench my thirst on your anger."

I did so, and cried out: "Agghhh! It's salty!"
The bloody taste made me gag, brought nausea.
I spat it out: an eye landed on a tree stump!
It seemed the weight of ruins collapsed on my shoulders.
Rain of blood fallen from my moon and Seven Sisters:
Horizon spread across my sight like Asia.

You were saying: "It's a grape…" And I was screaming:
"I see nothing but eyes upon the vines here!"

گفتی که انگور است

گفتی که "انگور است". گفتم: "نمی بینم".
گفتی که "باور کن! یک خوشه میچینم.
این باغ تاریخ است, وین تاکها هرسال
انگور میارند چندان و چندین..."

دستت تکان می خورد؛ انگارمی چیدی...
گفتنم: "ندارد راه شوخی در آیینم."
گفتی: "به هم نه چشم، وانگه دهان بگشا
تا بخشمت کامی زین ترد شیریتم."

من آنچنان کردم، گفتم که "وه! شور است!"
بیزاری قی بود زان طعم خونیتم.
افکندمش بیرون؛ برکنده چشمی بود!
گویی به سر بارید آوارسنگینم.
در دیده آقاقم، چون آسیا، می گشت:
باران خون می ریخت از ماه و پروینم...

می گفتی: "انگور است ..." فریاد من می گفت:
"بر تاکها، جز چشم، چیزی نمی بینم!"

MEHDI AKHAVAN-SALES

Mɛʜᴅɪ Aᴋʜᴀᴠᴀɴ-Sᴀʟᴇꜱ (1928-1990) was imprisoned
after the 1953 CIA-backed coup d'état, and his col-
lection *Zemestan* (Winter), published after his time in
prison, marked him as a major new poet. His other
collections, such as *Az in avesta* (From This Avesta)
and *Aakhar-e shah-nameh* (The End of the Book of
Kings), focus on early Persian myths.

THE RETURN OF THE RAVENS

At the threshold of dusk
on a greying bay
a thousand black boats sail past.

No sunlight, no moon.
On the water's glistening surface
a thousand crooning black boats.

See how the scene changes colour
dark-hearted firmament and luminous star.
Engulfed in the pitch-black sea
crystalline islands appear to an observer
black patches on a white shirt.

A thousand fellow-travellers of a day's comings and goings
a thousand beaks having washed away the marks of work
a thousand tight-browed fellow-travellers and comrades
a thousand rotting corpses and remains.

On a greying bay
at a time when day
is what we call "the past", and night "the future"
at a time when the sky is lightless, and the moon
absent, I witnessed
black stars
flying through the pallid
firmament, noisy black stars
in that low and crowded pallid sky.

بازگشت زاغان

در آستان غروب،
بر آبگون به خاکستری گرایانده،
هزار زورق سیر و سیاه می گذرد.

نه به آفتاب، نه ماه.
بر آبدان سپید،
هزار زورق آواز خوان سیر و سیاه.

یک ببین که چه سال رنگها بدل کرد؛
سپهرتیره ضمیرو ستاره ی روشن.
جزیزه های بلورین به قیرگون دریا
به یک نظاره شدند،
چو رقعه های سیه بر سپید پیراهن.

هزار همره گشت و گذار یکروزه،
هزار مخلب و منقار دست شسته ز کار،
هزار همسفر وهمصدای تنگ جبین،
هزار ژاغر پرگند و لاشه و مردار.

بر آبگون به خاکستری گراینده،
در آن زمان که به روز
گذشته نام گذاریم، و بر شب آینده،
در آن زمان که نه مهرست بر سپهر، نه ماه،
در آن زمان، دیدم
بر آسمان سپید،
ستارگان سیاه.
ستارگان سیاه پرنده و پرگوی؛
در آسمان سپید تپنده و کوتاه.

NOSRAT RAHMANI

Nosrat Rahmani (1929-2000) was born in Tehran. His poems were particularly popular with the urban youth prior to the Iranian Revolution. His collections include: *Kavir* (The Desert), *Shamshir, ma'shoogheye ghalam* (The Sword, the Pen's Beloved) and *Beeveye siyah* (The Black Widow).

EXILE IN A RING OF CHAINS

The city-fathers dragged an official shroud over the body
their gift
was a dazzling padlock.

The stench of our corpses
the stench of the corpses of our fathers and brothers wafted
                                        from beyond the door
the city-fathers said:
– A generation created
The corpses shrieked: It's a trick, a trick
It's death's profession!

The fish know
the depth of the fishpond equals the length of the cat's claw.

The earth is a cemetery;
and time
is old and stupid and deaf and blind.

Beyond the barricade of teeth there is no whispering
it's been a long wait since chains sprouted from throats
and tongues have rotted,
decomposing in mouths.

If I open the lips
blood and poison will spill out
Hey, prisoners, who will rise up now?
Which one of you?
Actually, it won't be insulting

تبعید در چنبر زنجیر

شهرداران کفن رسمی بر تن کردند
هدیه شان؛
قفل زرینی بود.

بوی نعش من و تو،
بوی نعش پدران و پسران از پس در می آمد
شهرداران گفتند:
- نسل در تکوین است
نعشها نعره کشیدند: فریب است، فریب
مرگ در تمرین است!

ماهیان می دانند،
عمق هرحوض به اندازه ی دست گربه است.

گورزاریست زمین؛
و زمان
پیر و خنگ و کر و کور.

در پس سنگر دندانها دیگر سخنی نیست که نیست
دیگرهیست که از هر حلقی زنجیری روئیده است
و زبانها در کام؛
فاسد و گندیده است.

لب اگر باز کنیم
زهر و خون می ریزد
ای اسیران چه کسی باز بپا می خیزد؟
چه کسی؟
راستی تهمت نیست

to ask: Are we the golden sons of captivity?
Doesn't it bother us that we're the warders of contempt?

A generation flaps its wings!

که بگوئیم: پسرها ی طلایی اسارت هستیم؟
و نخواهیم بدانیم نگهبان حقارت هستیم؟

نسلها پرپر زد!

FOROUGH FARROKHZAD

FOROUGH FARROKHZAD (1935-1967) was one of the most popular and influential modern Iranian poets. Her collections such as *Aseer* (Captive), *Deevar* (The Wall), and *Tavallodey deegar* (Another Birth) established her as the foremost female poet of her generation. A controversial figure, she was killed in a car accident in Tehran.

THE BIRD, ONLY A BIRD

Said the bird: "What scent, what sunshine
Ah, spring has arrived
and I'll go searching for a mate"

The bird departed: leapt from the edge
of the balcony, leapt like a message
the bird was tiny
the bird didn't think
the bird didn't read the newspaper
the bird had not taken out a loan
the bird was ignorant of humans

The bird, airborne over
the warning lights
was naively soaring higher
and ecstatically knowing
the blue moments

The bird, alas, was just a bird.

پرنده فقط یک پرنده

پرنده گفت: "چه بوئی، چه آفتابی، آه
بهار آمده است
و من به جستجوی جفت خویش خواهم رفت."

پرنده از لب ایوان
پرید، مثل پیامی پرید و رفت
پرنده کوچک بود
پرنده فکر نمی کرد
پرنده روزنامه نمی خواند
پرنده قرض نداشت
پرنده آدمها را نمی شناخت

پرنده روی هوا
و بر فراز چراغهای خطر
در ارتفاع بی خبری می پرید
و لحظه های آبی را
دیوانه وار تجربه می کرد

پرنده، آه، فقط یک پرنده بود

TAHEREH SAFFARZADEH

TAHEREH SAFFARZADEH (b. 1936) is a poet and translator, chosen as the 2005 Exemplary Personality by Afro-Asian Writers Organisation. Her collections include *Safar-e panjom* (The Fifth Journey) and *Deedar-e sobh* (Dawn's Visit).

FOG IN LONDON

fog is a native of London
a foreigner native in me
in winter, a tourist sees fog
then
zoo
then Tower of London

during evenings when I return to my room in Earl's Court
the fog-addicted road
blurs my recollection of where I have walked before
and stumbling I bump into the administrator's building;
in spite of a vast love for sun-drenched colonies
they pronounce my name incorrectly

Londoners cohabit with fog
and declare their passion
for sunshine;
one day you step onto a Tube platform,
anticipation of the city loop in your eyes,
to overhear people exclaiming:
such a lovely sunny day, isn't it?
you glance upwards,
the ceiling pressing down on your head

مه در لندن

مه در لندن بومی است
غربت در من
در زمستان توریست اول مه را می بیند
بعد
باغ وحشی
و برج لندن

غروبها وقتی به اطاقم در الز کورت بر می گردم
جاده ی مخدر مه
حافظه ی قدمهایم را مخدوش می کند
و من تلو تلو خوران ساختمان اداراتی را تنه می زنم
که با وجود عشق عظیمشان به مستعمرات آفتابی
اسم مرا غلط تلفظ می کنند

لندنیها به مه می زیند
و با آفتاب
عشق می ورزند
یکروز که روی سکوی مترو قدم می زنی
با انتظار خط کمربندی در چشمانت
مردم را می شنوی که به هم می گویند
چه روز آفتابی قشنگی اینطور نیست
تو به سوی بالا نگاه می کنی و می بینی
سقف دارد روی سرت فشار می آورد

AHMAD-REZA AHMADI

AHMAD-REZA AHMADI (b. 1940) was born in Kerman and educated at the Daar-ol-Fonoon college in Tehran. He has published over ten volumes of poetry, including *Rooznaame-ye sheeshe-ee* (The Glass Newspaper) and *Ghaafeeye dar baad gom meeshavad* (Rhyme Gets Lost in the Wind).

THE ABSENCE OF CONTACT

We must know all that occurs
the street has the aroma of summer
it's the season when they abandon cities under bombardment
little by little the east reaches the sea
a fish, out of the silence of seaweed, glimpses water...
The absence of contact...
we find each other in newspapers
we extract the odour of corpses from newspapers
and leave the light burning...
it's not the first time we have come to know
                "I" and "You" are allotted a place in the earth
we haven't walked in the rain
the wind howls distantly.

The absence of contact...
you could have worn blacker clothes
the snow blackens trees.

Nurses are attending the leafy funeral of our house
the windows gaping and I
                am, at last, ashamed of the scars

At last, I comprehend you
a journey ended in its own endlessness
a journey ended in the absence of contact...

And I only ask
           is Isfahan still fragrant with tiles?

کمبود تجربه های مشترک

همه چیز را باید بدانیم
راهرو بوی تابستان می دهد
فصلی است که شهرها را برای بمباران خالی کرده اند
شرق کم کم به دریا می رسد
ماهی،در سکوت خزه،آب را دوباره می بیند...

کمبود تجربه های مشترک...
ما یکدیگر را در روزنامه ها می بینیم
از روزنامه ها بوی اجساد را می پرسیم
و چراغ را روشن می گذاریم...
نخستین بر نیست که می دانیم
"من" و "تو" سهم زمین است

ما در باران قدم نزده ایم
دورتر از ما باد می آید.

کمبود تجربه های مشترک...
تو می توانستی لباس سیاه تر داشته باشی
برف درختان را سیاه می کند.

پرستاران به دفن برگهای خانه ی ما می روند
پنجره باز است و من
دیگر از زخم خجلم

من دیگر معنی ترا می دانم
سفری پایان یافته در نا تمامی خویش
سفری پایان یافته در کمبود تجربه های مشترک...

و تنها سئوال می کنم
آیا اصفهان هنوز بوی کاشی دارد؟

MIMI KHALVATI

Mimi Khalvati (b. 1944) was born in Tehran and grew up on the Isle of Wight where she went to boarding school. She has worked as an actor in the UK and as a director at the Theatre Workshop Tehran. Her collections of poetry include *Mirrorwork* and *The Chine*. Khalvati writes in English.

GHAZAL – AFTER HAFEZ

However large earth's garden, mine's enough.
One rose and the shade of a vine's enough.

I don't want more wealth, I don't need more lies.
In the dregs of a glass, truth shines enough.

What can Paradise offer us beggars
and fools? What ecstasy, when wine's enough?

Come and sit by the stream. Rivers run dry
but to carry their song, a chine's enough.

For a poet, browsing the old bazaar,
any book with a broken spine's enough.

When you're here, my love, what more could I want?
Just mentioning love in a line's enough.

As long as you live – wherever on earth –
no heaven however divine's enough.

I've no grounds for complaint. As Hafez says,
isn't a ghazal that he signs enough?

PARTOW NOORIALA

PARTOW NOORIALA (b. 1946) is a poet and literary
critic living in Los Angeles. Her collections include
Chahaar rooyesh (Four Springs) and *Az cheshm-e baad*
(Of the Eye of the Wind). She migrated from Iran to
the United States in 1986.

WOMAN

Shut my mouth
crush my hands
bury my thoughts
and hide me
clad in a black shroud
            in the darkest corner of the house.
I lived among others
in a realm of suspicion,
in a one-sided battle
estranged by estrangement
I made love in a prison,
and with an abandoned accent
sang songs of pain.

Now, you've become the vulture!
You've perched on my carcass,
but what will you do
            with the perfume of my charred bones?

Since I've experienced the fatigue of labour
amid fields of wheat
and the acrid stench of rice fields –
a child slung to my back –
I've scythed the root of my existence.

What will you do
            with my feeble eyes?
Since the frantic shriek of the factory
            has snatched me back to consciousness

زن

دهانم را ببندید
دست هایم را بشکنید
اندیشه ام را به خاک بسپرد
و پوشیده در کفنی سیاه
در تاریک ترین کنج خانه
پنهانم کنید.
در فضایی مشکوک
زیستم با دیگران
در نبردی نا برابر
جنگیدم با قداره بندان
در غربتی غریب
مهر ورزیدم در زندان
و با لهجه ای متروک،
ترانه خواندم از درد.

اینک ای کرکس پیر،
بر لاشه ام نشسته ای.
اما با بوی نیم سوخته ی استخوانم
چه خواهی کرد؟
که من خستگی کار را آموخته ام،
و در میان کشتزاران گندم
و بوی گس شالیزار،
- کولبار طفلم در پشت -
ریشه ی جانم را دور کرده ام.

با چشمان کم سویم
چه خواهی کرد؟
که من با سوت شتابزده ی کارخانه ها
به هوش آمده ام،

I've wound my life on a wheel
in that dungeon you call a "workshop".

What will you do
          with my bloodied fingers?
Since with every fresh pattern
I've planted
an old wound in the rug's garden.

What will you do
          with my devastated hands?
Since, proud and damaged,
I've wandered city streets
with a basket empty of bread,
and I've torn the huge blisters on my hands
while doing the laundry,
by cleaning and tidying the house
by cooking and serving,
awaiting the miracle of history.
What will you do with me?

You're basking in the shade of my misery;
you've woven a ragged noose of punishment
from the strands of my plaits
and with suspicion and doubt
you've called me insane and childish.
Shame on me for giving you life.

و در سیاهچالی به نام کارگاه،
زندگیم را چرخ کرده ام.

با انگشتان خونینم
چه خواهی کرد؟
که من با هر طرح نو در باغ قالی،
دردی عمیق را
بر زخم کهنه ام نشانده ام.

با دستان بلا دیده ام
چه خواهی کرد؟
که سال های سال،
با زنبیلی تهی از نان،
مغرور و زخم خورده،
از کوچه های شهر گذشته ام،
و دستانم را با داغ طاولی درشت
از شستشوی رخت،
از رفت و روب خانه
از پخت و پز،
در انتظار معجزه ی تاریخ
از هم گشوده ام.
با من چه خواهی کرد؟

در سایه ی رنج هایم یله دادی،
از تارهای گیسویم
ریسمان پوسیده ی قصاص بافتی
و مشکوک و تا باور
سفیه و کودکم خواندی،
شرمم باد که هستی ات دادم.

You sated your gluttonous appetite
on the flesh of my corpse
and poured the tragedy of lust
into my arteries
and enlisted my brother
   like Cain
with the allure of killing me.

Estranged and disturbed
you've made my life a grave,
and dropped the stones of chastity
on my head, and I saw
behind the stones' rain
your ashen face
   amidst the blush of spilt blood.
Brave and naive, I regret
having praised my murderer.

But executioner!
Bear history in mind
so come the morning of battle
I'll rise up like the phoenix, prepared.

اشتهای بی پایانت را
با موده ی تنم فرو نشاندی
و شوربختی شهوت را
در رگ هایم جاری کردی،
و آنگاه برادرانم را قابیل وار
به وسوسه ی کشتنم فرا خواندی.

مجنون و بیگناه،
زنده به گورم کردی،
و سنگ های نجابت را
بر سرم فرود آوردی.
و من از پشت باران سنگ،
چهره ی پریده رنگت را
به سرخی خون دیدم.
دریغا که بی باک و بی تدبیر،
قاتلم را ستایش کردم.

اما جلاد!
تاریخ را به خاطر بسپار،
زیرا که در صبحگاه نبرد،
ققنوس وار مهیا ی برخاستنم.

MAHMOUD KAVIR

MAHMOUD KAVIR (b. 1951) holds a PhD in Iranian History and Culture, and has been teaching for close to forty years. He has published more than twenty books, including collections of poetry such as *Toka khanoom* (Lady Finch) and *Azalia* (Azaleas).

COME WITH ME TO LEBANON

Hey you, offspring of moon and apple and olive!
I who wrote the Torah with musk
                    from the curls of Nazareth's daughters
I who braided Solomon's locks
with the narcissus of Sharon and the lilies of the valley!
I who made the fishing net
dance
with joy and passion!
I who perfumed Hira's cave
with the scent of kisses
How is it now
only tragedy befalls
his cave and this song?
Ah, which shameful envoy
has burnt the essence of love!

I am ablaze in the garden of deer
and pigeons;
feather by feather
the bird and the wings of Seyavush are burning; lost, lost, lost
may your name be lost
O war!

This lamp of shadowy eyes
this spring of tears
these olives of weeping
a narrow terrace of tears,
the shirts of wailing children.
Hey you, Jerusalem's daughters,

با من به لبنان بیا

آهای اولاد ماه و زیتون و سیب!
من که تورات را با مشک گیسوی دختران ناصره نوشته بودم
من که با نرگس شارون و سوسن وادی ها
گیسوی سلیمانم را بافته بودم!
من که تور را به شور
به سور
به رقص آورده بودم!
من که غار حرا را به بوی بوسه
خوشبو کرده بودم
اینک چگونه
بر این کوه و بر این کلمه
تنها رنج می بارد.
آه کدام نانجیب پیامبری
اینگونه آنش زد به جان عشق!

باغ کبوتر و آهو در آتش
و من
و بال بال سیاوش
و این پرنده ی آتش گرفته ی گم گم گم
گم باد نام تو
ای جنگ!

که چراغ!چشمه ی تاریکی
که چشمه، چشم اشک
که اشک های دربدر
زیتون های گریه؛
پیراهن کودکان
در شیون باد.
آی دختران اورشلیم

come and lament gazelles and deer of the desert
reed-fluted young women of hyacinth and saffron
come with me to Lebanon
from the peaks of Amanus
from the peaks of Hermon
O my sister O my bride
come with me
for we must sing a song for the murdered
we must recite a lullaby
without night or loss for the children.

شمار ابه غزال ها و اهوان صحرا سوگند
دوشیزگان سنبل و زعفران و نی
بیایید با من به لبنان
از قله های امانه
از قله های حرمون
ای خواهر و عروس من
بیایید
باید برای کشتگان ترانه ای بسراییم
باید برای کودکان
لالایی لیالی بی لیل و لا را بخوانم.

ALI ZARRIN

ALI ZARRIN (b. 1952) is a bilingual Iranian-American poet who immigrated to the USA in 1970. He graduated from the University of Washington with a PhD in Comparative Literature and is the author of ten books of poetry and literary criticism.

FREE GHAZAL (1)

Ah! I gasp inside my bright bubble.
Blister on my soul, and yet deep within, a balm forms.

At the other end of the line, a familiar voice
vanishes into eternity. At my end of the line, a tremulous

sound of harps echoing within my existence.
From the sky, the sounds of planes and choppers.

Television advertisements: Coca Cola, Travel to Jamaica,
First Grade Beef, Accident Insurance Lawyers, Orange Juice.

I breathe inside my bright bubble
and lapse into unconsciousness. I search inside myself

for the balm to soothe the blister on my soul,
                                the sound of the fan, of air,
a drop of perspiration moisturising my body

Ah, I burn and am relieved, I turn
and the world has spread its arms to embrace me.

At the other end of the line, a familiar voice
discovers me. At my end, I discover myself.

غزل آزاد (۱)

در درون حبابی روشن آه می کشم
تاولی بر روحم، اما مرهمی در درونم می جوشد

آن سوی خط تلفون، صدایی آشناست که در بی نهایت
گم می شود. این سوی خط منم که ارتعاش

صدا بر تار و پود وجودم طنین افکنده است.
از آسمان صدای هواپیما و هلی کوپتر می آید

تلویزیون تبلیغ می کند: کوکا کولا، سفر به جامائیکا
وکیل تصادفات، گوشت درجه ی یک، آب پرتقال

من در درون حبابی روشن نفس می کشم
و مدهوش می شوم، بر تاول روحم مرهم از ردون

می نهم، صدای پنکه، صدای هوا ست
و قطره های عرق بندم را نمور می کند

آه، می سوزم و لذت می برم، می گردم
و جهان آغوش خود را برمن می گشاید

از آن سوی خط تلفن، صدایی آشنا
مرا پیدا می کند، این سوی خط خود را می یابم

MAHASTI SHAHROKHI

Mᴀʜᴀsᴛɪ Sʜᴀʜʀᴏᴋʜɪ (b. 1956) is a poet, journalist and theatre critic. A graduate from the Fine Arts University of Tehran, she emigrated to France in 1984 and gained her PhD from the Sorbonne. Her novel *A Shawl as Long as the Silk Road* was published in 1999.

BEAUTIFUL WOUNDS

Come, see my wounds
See my smashed skull
See the spreading fractures
See the congealed blood
See my blooded larynx
See my slashed throat
See my torn uterus
See my ankles
See my fingers
See my elbows
See my bruised breasts
Look! Look me over
See these stains
All over me, do you see?
Do you see these wounds?

Nothing but wounds
Bruises
Congealed blood
Slashed throat
Torn uterus
Do you see?

Despite all of this, I'm still young and alive
And despite my smashed skull I'm still beautiful

زخمهای زیبا

بیا زخمهایم را ببین
ببین جمجمه ی شکسته ام را
ببین ترکها را اینجا و اینجا
ببین این خون مردگی ها را
ببین حنجره ی خونینم را
ببین حلق شکافته ام را
ببین زهدان از هم دریده ام را
ببین مچ پایم را
انگشتانم را ببین
ببین آرنجهایم را
ببین کبودی روی پستانهایم را
ببین! اینجا و اینجا را ببین
ببین این خراشها را
اینجا و اینجا را میبینی؟
می بینی این زخمها را؟

فقط همین زخمهاست
و این کبودیها
و این خون مردگی ها
و این گلوی پاره
و این زهدان از هم شکافته
می بینی اینها را؟

وگرنه من هنوز زنده ام و جوان
من هنوز زیبایم با این سر از هم شکافته

SHOLEH WOLPÉ

Sʜᴏʟᴇʜ Wᴏʟᴘᴇ́ (b. 1961) is author of collections of poetry such as *The Scar Salon* and *Rooftops of Tehran*, and is the associate editor of *The Norton Anthology of Modern Literature from the Muslim World*. Wolpé was born in Iran and lives in Los Angeles. She writes in English.

HIGH ABOVE TEHRAN

We are exiles, children of the dead
who melted into the earth without a trace.

And I, even at ten thousand feet see
this land as my home; bound. But look

the shadow of this plane flees too.

DAVOOD SALEHI

Davood Salehi (b. 1964) grew up in a village in the Fars province. He began writing in 1995 after returning to university. He has since written for a number of periodicals. He lives in Shiraz.

UNTITLED 3

iron birds
hideous vultures
rapid four-hoofed beasts
with those fierce colours
chafe at my heart
and I think about those birds singing songs in the wind
and the swallow returning each spring from its long migrations
            howling and screaming
is now perched expressionless in a plastic tree staring at me
high-altitude falcon from the killing field
is scenery on the wall
and a cannon-toting falcon
named Apache
its flight not for hunting rabbit nor for hunting deer
hunts land
hunts us
for one of us alone can survive
for us to die
it roars
the good old days of the hunter's falcon
the Apache and the man with a hand-grenade hidden in his heart
hunt us
and sow blood-soaked soil with landmines.

بدون عنوان ۳

پرندگان آهنی
لاشخورهای بی نوا
چهار پایان تندرو
با آن رنگ های تند
دلم را مالش می دهند
و یاد می کنم از پرندگانی که در باد ترانه می خواند
و چلچله هایی که هر بهار از گردشی دراز با داد و فریاد به خانه می آمدند
اکنون مبهوت نشسته بر درخت پلاستیکی و چشم دوخته است به من
شاهین بر فراز نخجیرگاه
چشم‌نگاره ای است بر دیوار
و شاهین بالگردی است توپدار
که نامش آپاچی است
و پروازش نه شکار خرگوش است و نه شکار آهو
شکار خاک و
شکار ما
برای ماندن یکی دیگر
برای مردن ما
غرنبش می کند
یادش بخیر شاهین نخجیر گر
آپاچی و مردی که نارنجکی در دلش پنهان کرده است
ما را شکار می کنند
و بر جایی می نهد بر خاکی خنونین.

FARZANEH GHAVAMI

FARZANEH GHAVAMI (b. 1968) was born in Tehran. Her collections include *Gofteh boodam man az nasl-e Shahrzad-ha-ye moztarebam* (I've Said I Belong to the Generation of Anxious Scheherazades) and *Az man faghat alangoo-yee meemaanad* (All That Remains of Me Is a Bracelet).

THE SAME EVENTS

My headscarf has flowered in corners of the sky
I divine the future through clouds
I decipher folds in the moon's face
time and again
she has lent her heart to a meteor shower

I rust behind the window
I paint
the last leaves of the plane tree
on a winter garden

My ice melts
down the drainpipe, filled with the sound of snow
I shriek from the rooftop

Between my eyebrows, a birthmark,
from which divination of full moons
predict the same events
that I decipher
I have not been enamoured of winter after winter
reading the newspaper behind the window
not
afternoons
it warms in my teacup
or otherwise
with ice
I divine the future through clouds.

تقویم های دوباره

من که روسری ام گوشه ی آسمان گل داده
فال ابرها را می گیرم
از چین های صورت ماه می فهمم
چندبار
دلش را به سنگ باران ستاره ها داده

من که پشت پنجره زنگ میزنم
آخرین برگ های این چنار را
روی زمستان حیاط
نقاشی می کنم

یخ هایم که آب شد
با ناودانی، پر از صدای برف ها
پشت بام را داد می زنم

خالی میان ابروانم است
که فال ماه های دنیا را
ازتقویم های دوباره می گوید
که می فهمم
چند زمستان را عاشق نبوده ام
که پشت پنجره روزنامه می خوانم
نه
بعداز ظهرها
در استکانم گم می شوم
یا هنوز
با یخ هایم
فال ابرها را می گیرم

MANDANA ZANDIAN

Mandana Zandian (b. 1972) is a poet and essayist.
She is the author of three books of poetry, including
Negaah-e aabee (Blue Sight) and *Hezar-tooye sokoot* (The
Labyrinth of Silence). She left Iran in 1999 and lives
in Los Angeles.

UNTITLED

You unlock the green
and whisper the geography of my body

I defeat you and myself
and am lost in both worlds

I've become "woman"
– exiled by your masculine presence

And the naked
song of my lips will document
history
in the red music of your flesh.

بدون عنوان

سبز را می گشایی
و نجوا می کنی جغرافیای اندامم را

فتح می کنی تو را و خودم را
و گم می شوم در هر دو جهان

"زن" شده ام
-- تبعیدی حضور مردانه ی تو

و تاریخ
سماع عریان لب هایم را
در موسیقی سرخ تنت
ثبت خواهد کرد.

ALIREZA BEHNAM

ALIREZA BEHNAM (b. 1973) is a poet and journalist living in Tehran. His collections include *Aghrabe-ha dor-e gord-baad* (Hands Over Whirlwind) and *It's my half that's burning*. He has worked as editor at a number of newspapers.

HANGING FROM THE TREES OF BABYLON'S TEMPLE

Finally, I shall plunge into my millennia
of existence
head over heels from the towers of Cheghaa-Zanbeel,
the ineffable compelling language's
leap to their parapets.
It's obvious that you will worship me
as ancient icon
hanging from the trees of Babylon's temple
Athens will see first light with me   and Paris   and
Persepolis
in countless tongues
shred me to bits
each bit orbiting your eyes with the zest of a word
sniggering with me
and the gravity of language towards Plato
and the flocks of Artemis
and the insurgency of separatist words.
All are within me
and I, into my millennia of existence
from virgins illumined on temple walls
to shadows splitting from your hard-drive
will be shattered
as all that's shattered is of me
you may ask
you may ask of me the future
I'll babble back the language of Babylon's people.

آویخته از درخت های معبد بابل

سرانجام به هیات چندین هزار سالگی ام
فرود خواهم آمد
وارونه از برج های چغا زنبل
و چیزی در من است که زبان را
به کنگره های برج پرتاب می کند
این روشن است که مرا بر خواهید کشد
به شمایل پیری
آویخته از درخت های معبد بابل
آتن در من طلوع خواهند کرد   و پاریس   و
پاسارگاد
و زبان های بیشمار
تکه پاره ام کنید
هر تکه ام به هیات واژه دور چشم های شما تاب می خورد
قهقهه در من است
و رویش زبان در آن سوی پلوتون
و گله های آرتمیس
و طغیان واژه های جدا از سر
این ها همه در من است
و من به هیات چندین هزار سالگی ام
از باکره های نقش بسته به دیوار معابد
تا سایه های جدا شده از رایانه های شما
پرتاب خواهد شد
و پرتاب شدگی در من است
بپرسید
از آینده بپرسید
به زبان مردم بابل جوام خواهم داد

BAHAREH REZAI

BAHAREH REZAI (b. 1978) was born in the province of Gilan and her first book *Anita, aroos-e chahaar fasl, sokoot* (Anita, the Bride of the Four Seasons, Hush) was published in 1998. She lives in Tehran.

48

Sometimes
we fail to uncover with a murmur
death chanting an anthem inside us
Sometimes
we fail to act out of love
with a tear
a dampness
on the face of a lover
on a rainy evening
we fail to understand a whisper of love
Sometimes, alone
in the middle of the night
with the call of an owl
we wake crazy
and weave fairy tales out of love.

۴۸

گاه
به زمزمه در نمی یابیم
مرگی که در ما سرود می خواند
گاه
به اشکی
نمی
بر گونه ی عاشق
در شبی بارانی
از عشق حرفی نمی فهمیم
در عشق کاری نمی کنیم
گاه، تنها
به صدای جغدی
در نیمه شبی
دیوانه بر می خیزیم
و از عشق، افسانه می بافم.

AHMAD ZAHEDI LANGROODI

Aʜᴍᴀᴅ Zᴀʜᴇᴅɪ Lᴀɴɢʀᴏᴏᴅɪ (b. 1982) writes film
and poetry criticism for periodicals such as *Kalak*
and *Naghde Noe*. His poem 'Eternal' won Iran's first
internet poetry prize in 2002. 'Dar bande daar' ('In
the Thread of the Noose') has appeared in print and
online.

THREAD OF THE NOOSE

The flower in the rug's
geometrical rhythm repeats
and when it touches the foot
the small girl has become a bride

Because of your absence
I stare at the sky
my life become like the vines.
Will the rain ever cease?

You draw thread on thread
through the weft, a jungle
against horizontal repetition, fabric
is one of the bride's possessions.

Did you know that you're weaving
over your face?
The rain is ceaseless.

I shut my eyes
and recall the repetition of a flower
you wove in the noose of the rug.

در بند دار

تکرار می‌شود، گل
در ریتم هندسی قالی
و تا پا بخورد
عروس شده دخترک

زندگی ام پیچک شده
از بس نیامدی و
چشمم خیره به آسمان است.
که باران بند می آید؟

و تو بند بر بند می کشی
از تار، جنگلی
و به تکرار افقی، پود
تا که اسباب عروسی باشد.

بند بر چهره می کشی
می دانی؟
این باران بند آمدنی نیست.

چشم هایم را می بندم
و تکرار گلی را به یاد می آورم
که بر دار قالی به بند می کشیدی.

ALI ALIZADEH was born in Iran in 1976 and migrated to Australia at the age of 14. He began writing in English in 1997 and received his PhD in Professional Writing from Deakin University, Melbourne in 2005. He has since taught writing and literature at universities in Australia, China, Turkey and United Arab Emirates, and is now a Lecturer in Creative Writing at Monash University, Melbourne. He is the author of six books including the collections of poetry *Ashes in the Air* (University of Queensland Press, 2011) and *Eyes in Times of War* (Salt, 2006); with Ken Avery, a book of translations of *ghazalyaat* of Attar from Farsi to English, *Fifty Poems of Attar* (re.press, 2007); the novel *The New Angel* (Transit Lounge, 2008); and the work of creative non-fiction *Iran: My Grandfather* (Transit Lounge, 2010).

JOHN KINSELLA's many volumes of poetry include: *The Silo: A Pastoral Symphony*; *The Undertow: New and Selected Poems*; *The Hunt*; *Peripheral Light: Selected and New Poems*; *The New Arcadia*; and *Shades of the Sublime & Beautiful*. He is also author of the critical works *Disclosed Poetics: Beyond Landscape and Lyricism*; *Contrary Rhetoric: Lectures on Landscape and Language*; and *Language and Activist Poetics: Anarchy in Avon Valley*. His previous plays are collected as *Divinations: Four Plays and Comus*. His other work ranges across genres from short fiction to novels, libretti to autobiography. He is a Fellow of Churchill College, Cambridge University and a Professorial Research Fellow at the University of Western Australia.

Other anthologies of poetry in translation published
in bilingual editions by Arc Publications include:

Six Slovenian Poets
ED. BRANE MOZETIČ
Translated by Ana Jelnikar, Kelly Lennox Allen
& Stephen Watts, with an introduction by Aleš Debeljak
NO. 1 IN THE 'NEW VOICES FROM EUROPE & BEYOND' ANTHOLOGY SERIES

Six Basque Poets
ED. MARI JOSE OLAZIREGI
Translated by Amaia Gabantxo,
with an introduction by Mari Jose Olaziregi
NO. 2 IN THE 'NEW VOICES FROM EUROPE & BEYOND' ANTHOLOGY SERIES

Six Czech Poets
ED. ALEXANDRA BÜCHLER
Translated by Alexandra Büchler, Justin Quinn
& James Naughton, with an introduction by Alexandra Büchler
NO. 3 IN THE 'NEW VOICES FROM EUROPE & BEYOND' ANTHOLOGY SERIES

Six Lithuanian Poets
ED. EUGENIJUS ALIŠANKA
Various translators, with an introduction by EugenijusAlišanka
NO. 4 IN THE 'NEW VOICES FROM EUROPE & BEYOND' ANTHOLOGY SERIES

Six Polish Poets
ED. JACEK DEHNEL
Various translators, with an introduction by Jacek Dehnel
NO. 5 IN THE 'NEW VOICES FROM EUROPE & BEYOND' ANTHOLOGY SERIES

Six Slovak Poets
ED. IGOR HOCHEL
Translated by John Minahane, with an introduction by Igor Hochel
NO. 6 IN THE 'NEW VOICES FROM EUROPE & BEYOND' ANTHOLOGY SERIES

Six Macedonian Poets
ED. IGOR ISAKOVSKI
Various translators, with an introduction by Ana Martinoska
NO. 7 IN THE 'NEW VOICES FROM EUROPE & BEYOND' ANTHOLOGY SERIES

Six Latvian Poets
ED. IEVA LEŠINSKA
Translated by Ieva Lešinska, with an introduction by Juris Kronbergs
NO. 8 IN THE 'NEW VOICES FROM EUROPE & BEYOND' ANTHOLOGY SERIES

Altered State: An Anthology of New Polish Poetry
EDS. ROD MENGHAM, TADEUSZ PIÓRO, PIOTR SZYMOR
Translated by Rod Mengham, Tadeusz Pióro *et al*

*A Fine Line: New Poetry from
Eastern & Central Europe*
EDS. JEAN BOASE-BEIER, ALEXANDRA BÜCHLER, FIONA SAMPSON
Various translators

*A Balkan Exchange:
Eight Poets from Bulgaria & Britain*
ED. W. N. HERBERT

*The Page and The Fire:
Poems by Russian Poets on Russian Poets*
ED. PETER ORAM
Selected, translated and introduced by Peter Oram

*Bones Will Crow:
15 Contemporary Burmese Poets*
EDS KO KO THETT & JAMES BYRNE
Translated by ko ko thett, James Byrne, *et al.*
with a preface by Ruth Padel
and an introduction by Zeyar Lynn

*The Parley Tree:
French-speaking Poets from Africa and the Arab World*
ED. PATRICK WILLIAMSON
Translated and introduced by Patrick Williamson

Please visit the Arc website for our full catalogue
of international poetry in translation

www.arcpublications.co.uk

www.ingramcontent.com/pod-product-compliance
Lightning Source LLC
Chambersburg PA
CBHW030827090426
42737CB00009B/909